language skills

Writing in Action

level **e**

LOYOLAPRESS.

Managing Editor	Kim Mason
Production Manager	Mary Bowers
Editors	Sandy Hazel, Jan Marcus, Margaret O'Leary
Production Staff	Phyllis Martinez, Kari Nicholls, Steve Straus
Interior Design	Mary Bowers
Cover Design	Alina Bravo

Acknowledgments

Every effort has been made to trace the ownership of all copyrighted material and to secure the necessary permissions to reprint selections. Any errors or omissions are unintentional and will be corrected in future printings.

Images copyright © Photodisc 1997.

ISBN 0-8294-1009-0

Printed by LSC Communications, Harrisonburg, VA,
USA, April 2018, Lot 042017

WRITING A MEMOIR

PREWRITING: What Is a Memoir?

In this unit, you will do some thinking about your life, and then shape an experience you have had into a kind of essay called a memoir.

Memoirs tell true stories about people's lives. From a memoir, you can learn how different lives can be. You can also discover what people learned from the experiences they have had.

As you write, you may find that you learn a little bit more about who you are and how you became that way.

You may write a memoir for yourself, but others will read it. Those people are your audience. Your audience will probably be your family or friends—the people you are "speaking" to as you write.

Here is an example of a memoir.

Coming Home Again

I was ten when my father came home one night and swooped up my mother in his arms. She started laughing, and so did he. "We're moving to Kansas City!" he yelled. They danced around and acted like it was the best thing that had ever happened. For me, it was the beginning of the worst time of my life.

We lived in Spokane, Washington. The sky there was the blue you see in those pictures of Africa in the *National Geographic* magazine, a blue that goes on and on. Sometimes I would just flop down on my back in the yard and stare up at the blue sky. I loved doing that.

Although I didn't realize it until we were about to move away, I loved a lot about Spokane. I loved the hours I spent with my best friend Andi, who was red-haired, freckled, always laughing, and always ready to climb a tree or run a race. I loved the steep hill at the top of the street that was closed off during snowstorms so we could all go sledding. I loved our old house, with the basement that smelled of dried fruit and heating oil, and the squeaky staircase that wound up to the second floor.

Most of all, I loved the cabin we had on the shore of a lake. The smell of sun on the pine needles was the most delicious smell in the world to me. It was a sharp, fresh smell that meant summer. On the shore of the lake, I would sit hidden by pine branches. The wind whispered through the branches, telling secrets that only I could understand.

And now, for some reason, my father wanted to give all this up. My father didn't often get excited, but there he was, dancing around with my mother, laughing and shouting, and all because we were going to leave Spokane.

As he told my mother all about the new job, his eyes shone and his fingers tapped the table. Her eyes were as bright as his, her red lips smiling. Neither of them seemed to care what I thought. Or if they did, they didn't ask me.

It's hard for me to remember the next couple of weeks of packing, cleaning, and getting ready to move. In my memory, it's all just a dull blur. But I do remember that when we backed the car down the driveway for the last time, my friend Andi ran after us. She put her hands on the window. "Best friends forever!" she shouted. I looked at the prints her hands made, and I believed her.

Kansas City was not Spokane. The sky was as gray as an old aluminum pan. There was no lake nearby. And there was no Andi. Sometimes I would see girls walking together, talking the way Andi and I used to, and I would feel like the loneliest person in the world. All I wanted was to go back to Spokane.

One day as I was sitting on the front steps by myself, a girl walked by with a big golden retriever pulling her on a leash. She was a skinny, short kid with white-blond hair and legs and arms that looked like white sticks. Her dog pulled her toward me, then he sat there with a big, goofy grin on his face.

"You new?" the girl asked.

I nodded.

"I'm Sarah," she said, "and this is Lance. It's short for…"

"Lancelot," I interrupted.

"Yeah," she said. "Like in the King Arthur tales."

"I'm Flora," I said. Then we didn't say anything more for a while. Lance sniffed at my hands and panted. I think he wanted to be friends. I wondered if Sarah wanted to be friends. I wanted to know more about her. But I couldn't think of anything to say.

Finally, Sarah muttered, "Well, I've got to go," and turned away. As she did, a book fell out of her backpack.

I bent down to pick it up. I couldn't believe what I saw.

"*A Wrinkle in Time*! I love that book!" I said, before I could stop myself.

Sarah turned around. "You do?" she said eagerly. "Me, too! Don't you love that part when that IT thing has Charles, and . . ."?

"And Meg is the only one who can save him?" I interrupted. She nodded and smiled, and for the first time since we'd moved to Kansas City, I began to smile, too.

Sarah sat down on the steps. We began to talk about the book, and about lots of other books, and it turned out she loved the same books I did. As we talked and talked, I scratched Lance behind the ears. He seemed happy. I know I was.

Before Sarah left, we made plans to take our dogs for a walk the next day. She said she would bring me a copy of a new book by Lloyd Alexander. And I promised to lend her my copy of *The Hobbit*.

That night, I went to bed happy, thinking about Sarah, who loved the same books I did. I thought about Andi, too. Back in Spokane, Andi and I had enjoyed great times playing outdoors, but we had never talked about books. I could see that Sarah was going to be a new kind of friend, not the same as Andi, but that didn't matter. I thought about change, and how hard it was to move. Then I thought about how good it felt to know I could make a new friend, someone who would make life in Kansas City as good as life had been in Spokane. For the first time, Kansas City felt like home.

Choosing a Topic

Some memoirs are as long as a book and tell about someone's entire life. A memoir like this may also be called an autobiography. Other memoirs focus on a shorter time or even a single event that was important to the writer. For example, E. B. White, the author of *Charlotte's Web* and *Stuart Little*, wrote a memoir called "Once More to the Lake." In this short essay, he tells about returning with his son to a lake he had visited every summer as a child.

You might not think that spending time at a lake is all that important. But it was to E. B. White.

That's what matters in choosing a topic for a memoir—that you write about an event that was important to you.

Now, brainstorm to make a list of three to five events that have been important to you. (You can list more events if you want.) They could be anything from getting a new puppy, to winning a prize, to the birth of a baby sister. Let your mind go back to things that happened to you that made you especially happy, sad, scared, or proud—something that stands out in your memory.

_____

_____

_____

_____

_____

_____

_____

_____

_____

_____

_____

Narrowing the Topic

You have a list of some events that have been important to you. Now take a look at what you wrote. Circle the ones that interest you most. Think about these questions:

- Which event meant the most to you?
- Which event do you think would be the most interesting for your audience to read about?
- Which event is narrow enough for a paper, but broad enough to be worth writing about?
- Which event taught you something?
- Which event are you most excited to write about?
- Which event do you think will make the best story?

Choose the Topic for Your Memoir

Now look again at what you circled and choose one event to write about. Write the topic of your memoir below.

My memoir will be about _____

_____

Freewriting for Your Memoir

Part of writing a memoir is remembering what you felt, did, and said. Think about:

- What happened?
- What sights, sounds, smells, or tastes come to mind?
- Why is this event important to you?
- What did you learn from it?

Sometimes the best way to start writing a memoir is to write everything you can remember about the event, without worrying about the order in which things happened, or what everyone said. On the lines below, take ten minutes and write what you remember about the event you will be writing about. Write freely and

quickly. Don't worry about anything except getting a lot of ideas and memories on paper.

_____

_____

_____

_____

_____

_____

_____

_____

_____

_____

_____

_____

_____

_____

PREWRITING: The Elements of a Memoir

In some ways, writing a memoir is like telling a story, the way you might tell a friend what happened when you went for a hike and got lost. A memoir often has many of the same elements as a story. Like a story, a memoir has:

- A plot—what happened (with a beginning, middle, and end)
- Characters—the people who are part of what happened
- A setting—where and when the event took place
- A theme—answers the question, "Why is this event important?" The theme tells the lesson you learned, or how the event affected or changed you.

To help you think about the elements of your memoir, fill in the blanks on this page. You will use these notes as you work on your memoir.

What are the main events? _Family mets on cruise and seven after having free icecream snorkling and so much more_

Who are the main characters? _Alana, Aubrey, Summer and rest of fam._

What is the setting? _The Royal Carribien from FL. to the bahamas and so forth._

What do you think the theme will be? _time to spend with family on Papas side_

Show, Don't Tell: Using Imagery

When you share a story with a friend, you want him to understand exactly what you felt and saw. The best writing is like that, too. It doesn't tell the reader what to think. Instead, good writing shows a reader what happened. It makes the reader feel like he is seeing a movie in his mind. You want to show your reader what you saw and experienced so that he, too, can see and experience it in his imagination.

Compare these two sentences:

> I loved the hours I spent with my best friend Andi, who was always happy and ready for action.

> I loved the hours I spent with my best friend Andi, who was red-haired, freckled, always laughing, and always ready to climb a tree or run a race.

The first sentence *tells* us about Andi. The second sentence *shows* Andi to us.

- The second sentence helps us see her: she is "red-haired" and "freckled."
- The first sentence tells us that Andi was "always happy," but the second sentence shows us Andi "always laughing."
- The first sentence uses the vague word "action." The second sentence shows us actions we can see in our mind: to "climb a tree or run a race."

When you get ready to write your draft, write a reminder for yourself at the top of the first page: "SHOW, DON'T TELL!"

Imagery

To help you show instead of tell, you can use imagery—language that appeals to the senses. Read this sentence aloud:

The sound of the locusts at night was loud.

You can tell you reader that a sound was "loud," but many sounds are loud. What makes this loud sound different from others? How can you show your reader what that sound was like? In his memoir called "Knoxville: Summer of 1915," the American writer James Agee wrote that the sound of locusts was

shivery in your flesh and teasing your eardrums, the boldest of all the sounds of night.

Imagery includes the sights, sounds, smells, tastes, or feelings that a writer creates in a reader's mind. Here is how E. B. White described being at a lake during his childhood:

I remembered clearest of all the early morning, when the lake was cool and motionless, remembered how the bedroom smelled of the lumber it was made of and of the wet woods whose scent entered through the screen.

Which words in that passage help you *see* and *feel* the lake? Which words appeal to your sense of smell?

As a grown-up, E. B. White went back to this lake and took his son with him. In his essay, White describes how he went on a fishing trip with his son that seems almost the same as the fishing trips he went on as a boy:

We went fishing the first morning. I felt the same damp moss covering the worms in the bait can, and saw the dragonfly alight on the tip of my rod as it hovered a few inches from the surface of the water. The small waves were the same, chucking the rowboat under the chin as we fished at anchor, and the boat was the same color green, and under the floor-boards the same wisps of moss, the rusty discarded fishhook, the dried blood from yesterday's catch.

Again, find the words that help you see, feel, hear, and smell what E. B. White experienced.

You can make a description more real for your reader by using imagery that *shows*. Look back at your freewriting. Find a scene or place that you can picture clearly in your mind. On the lines below, write two or more sentences that describe the place. Use as many images that appeal to the senses as you can.

_____

_____

_____

_____

_____

_____

Showing with Similes

Another way that you can show, not tell, is to use a *simile*. You might have learned about similes when reading poetry. A simile compares one thing to another thing using the words *as* or *like*: for example, "thunder like the booming of cannons," or "as quiet as a mouse."

When E. B. White visited the lake, here is how he described the sound of the outboard motors on boats:

> In the daytime, in the hot mornings, these motors made a petulant, irritable sound; at night, in the still evening when the afterglow lit the water, they whined about one's ears like mosquitoes.

Can you explain the simile in that sentence?

Now look back at the freewriting you did for your memoir.

• Name a place, person, or thing from your freewriting:

_____

• Write a simile to help show the person, place, or thing you chose:

_____

_____

_____

PREWRITING: Organizing a Memoir

When you write a memoir, you are telling a story. For many writers, the most natural way to organize a story is in chronological order—that means, to tell the events in the order in which they happened, from first to last.

The sample memoir on pages 1-4 mostly follows chronological order. It begins with an important moment in the writer's life in Spokane, Washington—the moment when the writer learns her family is moving to Kansas City. Then it moves back in time a little as the writer remembers what she loves most about Spokane. Then it starts moving forward again as the writer's family leaves Spokane. It ends with the writer in Kansas City after the move.

Look at the freewriting you did about the event you are writing about. Also look at what you wrote under "main events" on page 8. Now think about how you can organize the memoir you plan to write. Try using the chart on the next page to help you move from event to event in order. Below the main event in each box, write details that explain or describe the event. You do not need to use all the boxes. If you need to add more on a separate sheet of paper, that's fine.

1st Body

First event: Ariving at the cruise ship

detail Eating in the buffet because rooms were not ready.

detail got comfortable then met up at carosel

2nd Body

Second event: Activitys on the boat

detail The show "come fly with me"

detail The aqua show.

3rd Body

Third event: Activitys ooff the boat

detail Snorkling for shells.

detail shoping in the bahamas a little (knife for B'ed)

3rd Body

Fourth event: Nearly missing the boat of St. Maartin.

detail Stayed a ting bit to long b/c getting stuck in trafic

detail Running to and making the boat

DRAFTING: Writing the Body

Most essays have three parts:

- *The introduction*—the beginning, which gets the reader's attention and tells what the essay is about
- *The body*—the main part of an essay, which provides the information
- *The conclusion*—the ending, which wraps up the essay and makes readers feel as though they have learned something or read something satisfying

Many writers find that it is easiest to begin by jumping into the middle—the body of the essay. You have already done lots of planning to write the body. So, let's start with the body, and later go back to write the introduction and conclusion.

Before you begin to write, read and complete the exercises on the following pages.

What's Your Point of View?

The memoir called "Coming Home Again," which you read in Lesson 1, uses the pronoun "I." The writer refers to herself. She is the main character in her own story. She tells about her own experiences from her point of view.

When you use "I" in writing, you are writing in the *first person* point of view. In a memoir, you are telling a story about yourself, so it is fine to write in the first person. It makes sense to use "I."

In other kinds of writing, however, you probably would not use the first person. For example, if you write a report about history or science, you would not refer to yourself. Look at the articles on the front page of a newspaper. The writer tells about what happened, but doesn't refer to himself or herself. When the writer does not use "I," but instead uses "he," "she," "it," and "they," then we say the writer is using the *third person* point of view.

Fill in the blank:

1. Is the point of view of the following passage first person or third person?

_____

> When I was a little boy, I spent much of my time looking at the river. I liked to watch the ships as they came in with their white sails spread to the wind. I liked to think of the strange lands that they must have visited, and of the many wonderful things they must have passed.

2. Is the point of view of the following passage first person or third person?

_____

> Geese and other birds travel hundreds, or even thousands, of miles to warmer places in the south. They stay in the warm places until the spring. Then they return to their homes up north.

Circle the correct answers:

3. Which point of view would you use to write a report on history or science?

first person   *third person*

4. Which point of view do you use to write a memoir?

first person   *third person*

Watch Your Tense

Tense refers to time. A verb in the *present tense* tells an action happening now. A verb in the *past tense* tells an action happening in the past.

present tense	past tense
I walk.	I walked.
She jumps.	She jumped.
They dance.	They danced.

The memoir about "Coming Home Again" is written in the past tense. It begins: "I was ten when my father came home one night and swooped up my mother in his arms."

If that sentence were written in the present tense, it would read like this: "I am ten, and my father comes home one night and swoops up my mother in his arms."

Most memoirs are written in the past tense because the writer is telling events that occurred in the past. If you begin writing your memoir in the past tense, you need to keep using the past tense. You need to maintain *consistent verb tense*—in other words, do not switch back and forth between the past and the present tense.

Here is an example of a paragraph that switches tenses. Rewrite it so that it is all in the past tense.

When I got to the door of the huge department store, I was scared. I wanted to run away. Instead, I am strong. I square my shoulders, took a deep breath, and march right in there. I am not going to be scared by a building.

_____

_____

_____

_____

_____

Writing Dialogue

Try to include *dialogue* in your memoir. Dialogue is a conversation between two or more persons. When you write dialogue, you try to capture the way speech sounds. Dialogue is a good way of showing instead of telling. Contrast these two passages:

> My father was angry. He told me so, too. Then he told me to finish doing my chores before I asked him anything else.

> "Robert James! Come here, *now!*" I could hear my father from way out in the garage.
> "I'm coming!" I said, scrambling to get to him.
> "How many times do I have to tell you—" he began.
> "I'm sorry," I said quickly.
> "Don't interrupt!" he thundered. "And not another word! Finish your work. Now!"

The dialogue does a better job of showing what happened. It helps create the "movie" in your reader's mind.

If you are writing and find yourself writing *about* a conversation, then try instead to write it as a dialogue. Write the conversation just as you remember it. Keep in mind that most conversations do not take place in complete, well-formed sentences. When people talk, they often talk in phrases. Sometimes they don't complete what they are saying, or they are interrupted. You do not need to clean up the conversations you write. Write them just as they sound.

Look back at your notes for your memoir. Find a place where you could write a conversation. Now write the conversation here.

_____

_____

_____

_____

_____

_____

_____

_____

Ready to Write!

You have done all the preparation you need to write the body of your memoir. Gather all the materials you've already written:

- The chart you completed in the last lesson, to help organize your essay
- Your freewriting
- Your notes about similes
- Your notes about characters, events, setting, and theme
- Your dialogue

Look at the chart in which you described one event in each box. This is your guide to writing the memoir. Keep it by your side as you write.

Begin by writing a paragraph about the event listed in the first box. Then write another paragraph about the next idea or event. Each paragraph should focus on one idea or event.

Use what you have already written. When you get to the point where the dialogue fits in, add it. When you describe the character for whom you've already written a simile, add it. If you reach a point at which you're not sure what to write next, look back at your freewriting and other notes. They may help provide the words and ideas you need.

Keep going until you have written a first draft of the body of your memoir. Double-space when you write your draft. This will make it easier to revise later.

DRAFTING: Writing the Introduction

Congratulations! You have already finished most of the writing for your memoir.

Now it's time to write the beginning, or *introduction*. The introduction needs to make a good first impression on your reader. It should give your reader an idea of where you are headed with your writing, and it should make him want to keep reading.

Here is the introduction to "Coming Home Again," the memoir you read in Lesson 1:

> I was ten when my father came home one night and swooped up my mother in his arms. She started laughing, and so did he. "We're moving to Kansas City!" he yelled. They danced around and acted like it was the best thing that had ever happened. For me, it was the beginning of the worst time of my life.

Notice that the writer does not tell us, "I am going to tell you about when we moved from Spokane to Kansas City, and how hard it was for me." Instead, she shows us a dramatic scene. She puts us right in the middle of the action.

In the first sentences, we find out that the father and mother are excited, and we wonder why. By the end of the introduction, we know they are excited about moving, but the writer is not. The introduction lets us know the subject of the memoir—moving to Kansas City—and it makes us want to find out more about how things worked out for the writer.

There are several ways to begin a memoir. As long as your introduction manages to convince your reader to keep reading, and tells him a little about what to expect, you've done your job. Here are some ways to begin.

The Dramatic Situation

This type of introduction aims to grab your reader's interest quickly, in the first sentence or two. For example:

> When I saw my best friend slip the candy bar into her pocket at the store, I didn't know what to do or say.

That introduction immediately grabs the reader. What will the author do? Here is another example:

> When I saw Lindy running full tilt down the street, her legs a brown blur, I didn't have any idea that it would be five long days until I saw her again.

The reader wants to know what happened to Lindy. To find out, he will have to read on.

The Question

Sometimes you can interest your reader by beginning with a question. Here are two examples.

> Have you ever wanted something so much you couldn't stop talking about it, longing for it, even dreaming about it?

> What would you do if you woke up in the middle of the night and heard footsteps in the hallway?

Asking your reader a question is like engaging him in a conversation. He is instantly involved, and he usually wants to read on to find the answer to the question.

The Vivid Description

Sometimes, a place, person, or possession is central to a memoir. You can begin your memoir by describing that important place, person, or possession. Here are two examples:

> One of her ears had a piece bitten out of it, and her head was always at an angle, as if to say, "What do you think?" Her brown and black fur always looked dirty, as if she had just come up from a satisfying roll in a mud puddle. She had brown eyes that looked like melted chocolate.

> This house looked more than spooky. Thick, tangled vines greedily climbed the red brick walls. Jagged edges of broken glass glinted in the windows. The front door, swinging slowly on its hinges, seemed like the dark mouth of some hungry creature. And the big sign in the front yard, saying "KEEP OUT," just seemed to be begging Robert and me to enter.

A Sense of Humor

If you can start by making your reader smile or laugh, you will make him want to keep reading. Here is the opening sentence from a memoir by one of America's greatest writers, Mark Twain:

> Fifty years ago, when I was a boy of fifteen and helping to inhabit a Missourian village on the banks of the Mississippi, I had a friend whose society was very dear to me because I was forbidden by my mother to partake of it.

We smile at the idea of a friend who is "very dear" because the writer was forbidden to see him. Here are the first two sentences from E. B. White's "Once More to the Lake":

> One summer, along about 1904, my father rented a camp on a lake in Maine and took us all there for the month of August. We all got ringworm

from some kittens and had to rub Pond's Extract on our arms and legs night and morning, and my father rolled over in a canoe with all his clothes on; but outside of that the vacation was a success and from then on none of us ever thought there was any place in the world like that lake in Maine.

When we imagine the father in the water with all his clothes on, we chuckle in spite of ourselves.

If you want to use humor in your introduction, you don't have to tell a wildly funny joke. All it takes is a touch of wit to win over a reader.

Write Your Introduction

Read through the first draft of the body of your essay. You may find that, with some changes, the first paragraph will work well as an introduction. More likely, you will want to write a new paragraph for your introduction.

Think of what your approach should be. Will you try a dramatic situation, a question, a vivid description, or some other way?

On the lines below, write your introduction. Remember to:

• Grab your reader's attention.

• Give your reader a sense of what your memoir will be about.

_____

_____

_____

_____

_____

_____

_____

DRAFTING: Writing the Conclusion

The conclusion of a memoir serves two purposes:

- It satisfies the reader. When a reader finishes a piece of writing, he wants to feel that the loose ends have been tied up. You might think of this as closing the circle that begins with the introduction, moves through the body, and finishes with the conclusion.
- It tells what you learned. A memoir should have a theme—something you learned, whether it is a new understanding about yourself, others, or the world. In the conclusion, you can tell your reader what you learned. The theme doesn't have to be deep or heavy with seriousness. You might have learned, like Dorothy in *The Wizard of Oz*, that there's no place like home.

Here is the conclusion to "Coming Home Again," the memoir you read in Lesson 1:

> That night, I went to bed happy, thinking about Sarah, who loved the same books I did. I thought about Andi, too. Back in Spokane, Andi and I had enjoyed great times playing outdoors, but we had never talked about books. I could see that Sarah was going to be a new kind of friend, not the same as Andi, but that didn't matter. I thought about change, and how hard it was to move. Then I thought about how good it felt to know I could make a new friend, someone who would make life in Kansas City as good as life had been in Spokane. For the first time, Kansas City felt like home.

When you read that conclusion, you feel satisfied. The writer has tied up the loose ends and closed the circle of the move from Spokane to Kansas City. You also know what the writer has learned from her experience: that she can make new friends and be as happy in her new home as she was in her old one.

Reread the introduction and body you have written so far. Sit and think a minute about how you want to tie up the loose ends in your memoir. Also think about the theme you want to communicate to your reader.

On the lines below, make some notes about your theme. You don't have to write it perfectly—just write some words, phrases, or sentences to help you figure out what you want to say.

What is the theme I want to leave with my reader?

_____

_____

_____

Now you're ready to write your conclusion. Use the lines below to write a first draft.

_____

_____

_____

_____

_____

_____

_____

_____

Revising the Memoir

You have written a complete first draft of your memoir, with an introduction, body, and conclusion. Now it's time to revise—to make your essay as good as it can possibly be.

In revising, you might change the order of some paragraphs. You might add more details. You might take out some sentences.

Let's begin by looking at the content and organization of your essay.

The Big Picture: Content and Organization

When you revise, first look at the big picture. Don't worry about spelling or punctuation right now. Instead, focus on the *content*—the main points in your essay. Also consider the *organization*—the order in which you present the main points.

Content: Reread what you have written. Did you make every important point you want to make? Did you leave out any important scenes or ideas? If so, add them now. If you need to add a paragraph, write it on a separate sheet of paper, and make a note on your draft, such as, "Insert new paragraph here."

You may also find that some of what you wrote is unnecessary. If so, draw a line through the unnecessary words or sentences.

Organization: Some writers find that after writing their first draft and reading it over, they need to reorganize their work. For example, they might need to move a paragraph near the end back to the middle or the beginning. Remember, if you rearrange paragraphs, you may need to change some words to make the essay read smoothly.

Do the events make sense in the order in which you write about them? Can a reader easily follow what you have to say?

Think of your memoir as a story. Is there a clear plot, in which events lead from one to another? Is there a beginning, middle, and end?

Paragraphs: Focus, Details, and Transitions

Focus: Look at each paragraph in turn. Does each paragraph focus on one event or idea? You may find short paragraphs that you should combine, or a long paragraph that you should break into two or more paragraphs. Keep in mind that each paragraph should focus on one main event or idea. (Note: This doesn't apply to passages of dialogue, in which you begin a new paragraph each time the speaker changes.)

Details: Within each paragraph, ask yourself if you provide enough detail. Details help turn the story on the page into a movie in the reader's mind. When you think about details, focus on:

- *The people (characters)*: Do you feel you have described them well? Are there places where you could add details to help your reader understand your characters better, perhaps by adding an adjective, describing what a character's reaction was, or showing what she was doing? Look at the details in these descriptions from "Coming Home Again":

    I loved the hours I spent with my best friend Andi, who was red-haired, freckled, always laughing, and always ready to climb a tree or run a race.
    She was a skinny, short kid with white-blond hair and legs and arms that looked like white sticks.

- *The place (setting)*: Place is important in a memoir. Can you add details to help your reader see, smell, or hear the place you are writing about? Consider the details in these descriptions of the settings in "Coming Home Again":
    The smell of sun on the pine needles was the most delicious

smell in the world to me. It was a sharp, fresh smell that meant summer.

Kansas City was not Spokane. The sky was as gray as an old aluminum pan.

Transitions: Transitions help readers move smoothly from paragraph to paragraph and from sentence to sentence.

From Paragraph to Paragraph: To help your reader move through the events in your memoir, use transitional words and phrases. These often begin a paragraph, for example:

- *The next morning*, as we were getting ready to leave, I saw her again.
- *Another* challenge now faced us—how could we cross the river when the bridge was washed out?
- *Although* I didn't realize it until now that we were about to move away, I loved a lot about Spokane.

From Sentence to Sentence: You may be writing about a series of events in a paragraph. Transitional words help your reader keep track. You can use words such as *first, next, now,* and *last* to show your reader where he is in the story. For example:

- *First*, we had to carry the box secretly out the front door. *Then* we had to find a place to hide it.
- *Before long*, the bus arrived.
- *Finally*, Sarah muttered, "Well, I've got to go," and turned away.

As you read through your draft, add transitional words or phrases wherever you think they will help your reader better understand what's going on.

Sentences: Active Voice

Compare these sentences:

Paco hit the ball deep into the outfield.
The ball was hit deep into the outfield.

The first sentence is written in the *active* voice. The second sentence is written in the *passive* voice.

In the first sentence, you can clearly tell who is doing the action. Who hit the ball? Paco did.

In the second sentence, it's not clear who is doing the action. Who hit the ball? The sentence doesn't say.

Here is a sentence in the passive voice. Try rewriting it in the active voice. (You can decide who is doing the action.)

The scared kitten was rescued from the burning building.

_____

Almost always, try to write in the active voice. Read the following sentences. Write whether each sentence is active or passive. If the sentence is passive, rewrite it to make it active. If it is not clear who is doing the action, you can decide who is doing it.

1. The meal was cooked by Roberto. _____

_____

2. Shanice and I visited her mother. _____

_____

3. A concerto was played by the symphony orchestra. _____

_____

4. Bill was given a birthday party by his friends. _____

_____

5. The door was slammed. _____

_____

6. Charles Dickens published his books first in magazines. _____

_____

7. Henry and Carly were told by their aunt not to leave the room. _____

_____

8. Harriet remembered to lock the door. _____

_____

Is there ever a good reason to use the passive voice? When you don't know who did the action, or when you want to emphasize who received the action, you can use the passive voice. Here is an example:

Henderson was elected president yesterday.

The important thing in that sentence is Henderson's election, not who elected him. So the passive voice works in that sentence. In most cases, though, you will want to use the active voice.

Go through your draft and see if you can identify any sentences in the passive voice. If you find any, try to make them active.

Words: Precise, Vivid, and Concrete

Precise, vivid words. Use words that are precise instead of vague. Precise words show your reader what you want him to see. The noun "doctor" shows more than "man," just as "golden retriever" shows more than "dog." The verb "grasped" shows more than "got." The adjective "gentle" shows more than "nice." Look at your words to make sure you have used the most precise words you can.

Concrete nouns. Use concrete rather than abstract nouns. You can see and touch a concrete noun; an abstract noun is an idea. If you use a concrete word, your readers will be more likely to have the same image in their minds as you do.

In his essay "Once More to the Lake," E.B. White uses the abstract noun "debris" to describe what is in the bottom of the boat, but then adds concrete nouns that help us see what he means: "the wisps of moss, the rusty discarded fishhook, the dried blood from yesterday's catch."

Take a final look at your memoir. Does it express exactly what you want it to, in the best way you can? If it does, you have finished your revision.

Proofreading and Publishing the Memoir

You've reached the final steps of writing your memoir. Now it's time to *proofread*. When you proofread, you are a detective looking through a magnifying glass, trying to catch even the tiniest error in grammar, punctuation, or spelling.

You can use these proofreading marks to show how you want to fix each error:

Mark	Meaning	Example
⁋	Start a new paragraph	preferred. ⁋An emotional man
℘	Delete (take out)	store.℘ An old man of sixty
∧	Insert (put in)	as opened the door
⌒	Delete space	store. An old ⌒ man of sixty,
#	Add space	store. An old#man of sixty,
⬭	Misspelled word	(stoar.) An old man of sixty,
∽	Switch places	store. An man old of sixty,
⊙	Add period	store⊙ An old man of sixty,
⌃	Add comma	An old man of sixty, he was
⌄	Add apostrophe	sitting in Joes candy store
≡	Capitalize	store. an old man of sixty,
/	Use small letter	store. An Øld man of sixty,
↶⬭	Move circled word to point of arrow	store. An man of sixty (old)

Proofread for Grammar

Look for any errors in grammar. For example, did you write complete sentences? Did you use a plural verb with a plural subject? Do you need to rewrite any of your sentences because they are incomplete or run-on?

Proofread for Word Usage

Make sure that every word you use is the right word. Double-check for tricky words that sound alike but are spelled differently (homophones), such as *there* and *their*, or *two*, *too*, and *to*.

Proofread for Capitalization

Did you begin each sentence with a capital letter? Did you capitalize all proper nouns? Did you capitalize the pronoun "I"?

Proofread for Punctuation

Check end punctuation marks such as periods and question marks. Check for correct use of commas and apostrophes. If you wrote dialogue, double-check your use of commas and quotation marks to make sure you got it exactly right.

Check for Spelling

Even if you are using spell-check on your computer, errors can creep in. For example, the computer won't tell the difference between *passed* and *past*. If you have a question about a word, use a dictionary to check the spelling.

Publishing

After you have made all your corrections, make a fresh copy of your memoir. Share it with relatives and friends.

This essay is a record of something important to you, so you might want to make it into a book to keep. It's a piece of work you will want to look back at when you are older, both because it shows your best writing and because you will find it interesting to see what you thought when you were this age.

WRITING A RESEARCH PAPER

Choosing a Research Paper Topic

You have probably already written a report. Maybe it was about an animal or a famous inventor. A *research* report is also about a nonfiction topic—that is, it contains facts and is about something real.

A research report, though, probably goes deeper than the reports you may have written. One difference is that you have an idea about the topic. You do research in several books or magazines to find facts that support your idea. Then you use those facts to write your research paper.

People at work often write research papers. For example, imagine you work in a publishing company. You might write a research report on what is happening in the book business. You might write a report on new books that are being published elsewhere. You will use the researching and writing skills you learn long after you have finished writing this report.

In a RESEARCH PAPER, a writer collects, organizes, and reports the work of others to support a particular idea.

The topic of your research paper may or may not be a recent development. It can be almost anything in which you have an interest. When Trish thought about some subjects that fascinated her, she listed the following:

1. music videos
2. football
3. space exploration

✓ On the lines below, list three subjects that interest you a great deal or about which you'd like to learn. Don't worry about whether the subjects are suitable for a research paper.

1. _____

2. _____

3. _____

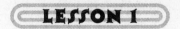

PREWRITING: Selecting a Topic

To enjoy writing a research paper, it is important to choose a topic that truly interests you. There are also some other requirements to keep in mind.

Selecting a person is probably not a good idea. Jeff wanted to write about a famous basketball player he admired. When he started his research, however, he couldn't find enough information for a paper. All of the articles he found repeated the same few facts. Jeff's big brother suggested that he write about some other aspect of basketball and he quickly agreed. Jeff put "Basketball" on his of possible topics. Use the questions below to help you think about a topic.

What subjects interest you? _____

_____

What activities do you enjoy? _____

_____

What do you wish you knew more about? _____

_____

☑ Using the list you made on page 35 and your answers to the questions above, list some possible topics for your research paper:

_____

_____

Zooming In on Your Topic

If your topic is too broad, you won't be able to cover it in one research paper. If it is too narrow, you won't be able to find enough information. Jeff's first idea, "A Famous Basketball Player," was too narrow; he couldn't find enough information. His second topic, "Basketball," was too broad. Jeff narrowed his topic to "The History of Basketball."

A. Below are some topics. Put a check mark next to those you think would make good research papers. Put *B* beside topics that are too broad, and *N* beside those that are too narrow.

_____ trees   _____ science

_____ the Japanese maple tree   _____ Halley's Comet

_____ fashions in the 1970s   _____ natural disasters

_____ your favorite musician   _____ the universe

B. One good way to narrow your topic is to think of a specific question about it that you would like to have answered. On the lines below, list again the topic ideas you chose on page 36. Then write a question you would like to have answered about each topic. For example, see Jeff's topic and question on the first line.

Topic   **Question**

1. *Basketball*   *How and when was basketball invented?*

2. Appleloosa   What makes the appalosa unique?

3. _____   the History of the appalosa

4. Mars   what makes mars unique

☑ Put a star ★ next to the question that interests you most. Next, write your question in the form of a topic. For example, Jeff's question, "How and when was basketball invented?" became his topic, "The History of Basketball."

"The history behind Niagra falls"

Think of this topic as your *working* topic, not necessarily the one you'll decide to write on after you've done some research. One of the secrets of research is changing your topic to fit the information you find. A good researcher molds and adjusts the topic to match his or her research notes. If your topic doesn't work out at all, you'll have two other topics (from your list above) to which you can turn.

PREWRITING: Following the Right Steps

A research paper is a big project. It could be discouraging if you plunged right into the middle. The secret is to take one step at a time in the proper order. Below is a checklist that will help you. As you research and write your paper, come back to this page and check off each step that you complete. (Start at the bottom.)

The Right Steps

_____ CONGRATULATIONS! YOU DID IT!

_____ Prepare the final copy.

_____ Prepare a bibliography.

_____ Revise your paper.

_____ Write your first draft.

_____ Make an outline.

_____ Write a thesis statement.

_____ Organize your notes.

_____ Take plenty of good notes.

_____ Fill out a bibliography card for each source.

_____ Make a list of possible sources.

√ Choose and narrow a topic.

Using the Library

Don't let the library overwhelm you. The information you need is not difficult to find if you know where and how to look. This lesson and the next one will help you do your research efficiently, so that you can save time and avoid backtracking. Good luck and good researching!

The library has three main resources that you will need to use: circulating books, magazines and other periodicals, and reference materials.

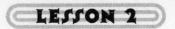
A. **Circulating books.** These books may be borrowed from the library. Libraries divide circulating books into *fiction* and *nonfiction*.

1. Fiction books are arranged in alphabetical order on the library shelves by each author's name, last name first.

2. Each nonfiction book has its own catalog number, which is written on its spine. If you know the catalog number of a book, you can find it by following the signs posted in your library.

Finding Books

When you need a book for your research, begin by looking in the library catalog. A library lists its books and other holdings in its catalog. Most libraries now list their books and other sources in a computer catalog, but some libraries still use a card catalog.

Card Catalogs

Card catalogs list books by subject, title, or author. To find a book on bluebirds, for instance, you would look in the catalog that lists subjects beginning with *B*.

A card you found in that search might look like this. Notice what each part of the card means.

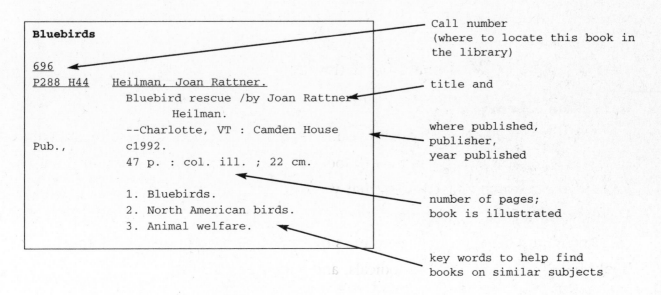

Computer Catalogs

Most libraries today use computers to store information about their books and other holdings. Most computer catalogs give you instructions on the screen for how to use the catalog. Usually, you can search by keyword, author, subject, title of the book, or you can "Search all Categories." When you search by keyword, the computer looks for any of the other types of entries with that word in it. Here is a book the computer might find for a keyword request about butterflies. Notice what each part of the entry means.

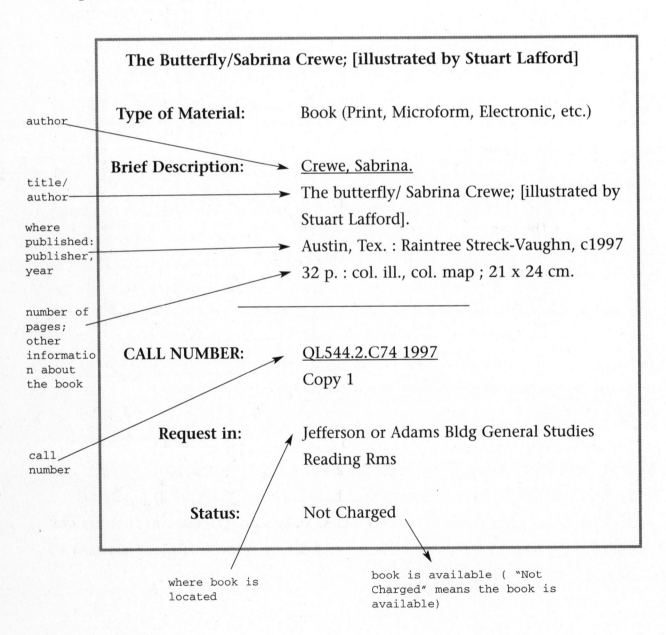

Finding Magazines

Magazines often have information in articles that researchers can use. There are two ways to find magazine articles on your topic. One is a published magazine index such as the *Reader's Guide to Periodical Literature*. This index is published throughout the year and also in hardbound yearly editions. The *Reader's Guide* lists articles alphabetically by both subject and author.

Unless you know the subject you are researching would have been written about in a particular year, begin with the most current edition of the *Reader's Guide* and work backward. If you find a magazine article that looks promising, write the information you will need to find it in your library. You may want to have a list of the magazines your library carries with you as you work. Before you copy information about an article, check that your library has the magazine. Here is the information you will need:

- The title of the magazine
- The volume number and publication date of the magazine
- The name of the article and its author
- The pages on which the article appears

Today, many libraries' magazine holdings are in a computer database. Usually, you can look up a subject, an author, or the title of an article. When you find an article in the database that looks useful, copy the same information about the magazine as you would if you used the *Reader's Guide*.

However you find articles you want to look at, ask your librarian to help you locate them in the library. Sometimes, the articles will be stored right on the computer, and you can print them to take home. If the articles are in magazines, you will be able to make copies of the articles. Make sure you also copy the page of the magazine that tells the name, volume, and date (look at the pages right after the Table of Contents for this information).

Finding Reference Materials

Reference materials include encyclopedias, dictionaries, indexes, almanacs, and other special books that you cannot check out of the library. When you are using a reference book, you will want to look up your subject as it is listed alphabetically. If you cannot find it there, look in the index of the reference book to see where the information on your topic is located. In some books, such as almanacs, the index is in the front.

Finding Information on the Internet

Today, more and more research takes place on the Internet. Here are some guidelines for getting the most out of this resource.

Use a Search Engine

A search engine looks among the millions and millions of sites on the Internet to find information that matches what you are looking for. Let's say you were researching where polar bears live. After you connect to the Internet, type in the address of a search engine into the address box at the top of the screen. One of the easiest search engines to use is Google. You can reach Google by typing www.google.com in the address line.

Type in Precise Words

Make your request as specific as you can. A search such as *bear* will pull up a huge number of responses. A request such as *polar bear habitat* will show you entries that may be more helpful.

Be Careful!

When a publisher decides to print a book or magazine, the publishing company has decided that the information is well-researched and worthwhile. That isn't the case with the Internet. Anyone can put anything in a website. Museums or universities sponsor some websites. But other websites are created by people who think they have something to say. Be very careful before you decide to use the information in a website. Check to see whose website it is. If you are not sure you

can trust the information, ask a librarian or adult. If you still have any doubts about the website, don't use information from it.

To check your understanding of sources, answer the following questions.

1. Where would you look for a novel by Mark Twain?

_____

2. What are three places you could find information for a research paper on the way the Hopi Indians lived 100 years ago?

_____

_____

_____

3. How would you find books written about the author Laura Ingalls Wilder?

_____

_____

4. Where would you find a map that showed the natural resources of India?

_____

PREWRITING: Exploring Sources

Now it is time to explore the library to see what information is available on your topic. Before you begin, take a minute to review the three main kinds of library materials and the facts you'll need to find them on the shelves.

Source	Where to Look	Facts Needed to Find
1. Circulating books	Card catalog or computer catalog	call number, title, author
2. Magazines	*Reader's Guide* or computer catalog	title, volume number, publication date, page numbers
3. Reference materials	Card catalog or computer catalog	call number, title, volume number, page numbers

Preparing a List of Sources

The purpose of this step is to narrow the huge number of sources available in the library to a much smaller number that you can easily manage. This activity requires some detective work. In order to complete it, you must go to the library and search out sources of information on your topic. Once a source is found, write down the facts you will need (see the chart above) to find it again when it is time to take notes. Each time you find a source, record the information necessary to relocate it. Here is an example of a listing for a source of information about hurricanes:

030 *Encyclopedia Americana,* Vol. 14, pages 613–14

☑ Use the lines below to list sources you find for your topic.

_____

_____

_____

_____

_____

_____

When you have finished this first research step, you should have a list of at least five sources that may contain information on your topic. The next step is to go back to each source you've listed to see if it is one you'll be able to use.

Preparing Bibliography Cards

Begin by taking a packet of file cards and your list to the library. Start with the first source on your list. When you have found it, scan it briefly to see if it discusses your topic. *If it does*, stop and fill out a BIBLIOGRAPHY CARD for this source, using one of your cards. *If it does not*, omit it and go on to another source.

Your bibliography card should look like this:

Call number	*510.432*
Author	*Alexander, Kenneth*
Title	*How Your Government Works for You*
Publication facts	*New York: Duffy and Co., 1964*

Below is a list of information that bibliography cards for different kinds of publications must contain:

1. Books: call number, author's name, title, city of publication, name of the publisher, and date of publication

2. Magazines: author (if known), title of article, title of magazine, volume number, date of publication, and page numbers

3. Encyclopedias (and other sets of books): author (if known), title of article, title of encyclopedia, volume number, and pages

☑ Fill out a separate bibliography card for every source you use in your research. It is important to record all of this information. If you don't, you will have to waste time backtracking later.

PREWRITING: Taking Notes

Now that you have found sources to use in your research, what do you do with them? The answer is, "Take notes properly, in order to avoid plagiarism." PLAGIARISM occurs when a writer uses the written words or ideas of a published author without giving proper credit. It is a form of stealing that you must avoid.

Later, you will learn how to give proper written credit to the author of material you use in your research paper. Right now, however, concentrate on taking good notes.

Students sometimes make the mistake of writing down every word they read. This process takes far too much time and energy. Here is a much better technique.

_____ 1. At the top of a new file card, identify (by title or author) the source you have chosen. Then begin to read the source.

_____ 2. Indicate at the top of the card the specific type of information you are recording (for example, "History of Pyramids").

_____ 3. As you read, summarize the information you have found by putting it into your own words. You don't have to write in complete sentences. In fact, it is better to take notes in phrases. On each note card, indicate the page number on which you found the information.

_____ 4. Write only one main idea per card.

The process of reading material and then summarizing it in your own words is called PARAPHRASING. Compare this paragraph with the note card at the top of page 47 to see how Mac paraphrased some information about pyramids.

> We do not know for certain how pyramids were built, but it is most likely that ramps were used, up which the stones could be dragged on sledges to each succeeding level of the pyramid by the multitude of workers employed on the project. These workers would have been drawn from among the peasants who would have been available in large numbers at the time of the annual flooding of the Nile, when they would have been unable to cultivate the fields.
> Leacroft, Helen and Richard. *The Buildings of Ancient Egypt.*
> (New York: William R. Scott, Inc., 1963), p. 9.

Mac's note card looked like the one below.

> *Building the Pyramids*   *Leacroft, p.9*
>   *Workers probably dragged*
>   *stones up ramps.*
>   *Workers mostly peasants —*
>   *many available when Nile flooded.*

Practice Taking Notes

Read the following paragraph. Then follow the four steps on page 46 to prepare a note card. Use the box below for your practice note card.

The Egyptians did not use horses because there were none in Egypt in those early days. There were other animals that might have been used to drag stones, but the Egyptians did not have the equipment to harness them properly. The only kind of harness the early Egyptians had was a loop that fitted over an animal's neck. If an animal was forced to drag a heavy load, this sort of harness would choke it. Under such conditions a man was a much more efficient beast of burden.

Cohen, Daniel. *Ancient Monuments and How They Were Built.*
(New York: McGraw-Hill, 1971), page 34.

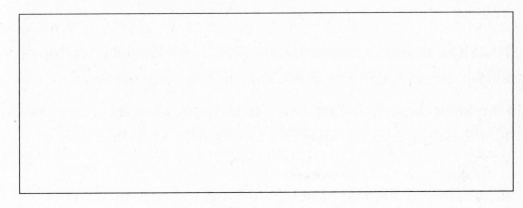

✔ Use the model above and the checklist on page 46 as you complete the first few note cards for your own research. Be sure that each card contains the name of the author and the specific page number where the information is located. If you use the author's exact words, enclose these words in quotation marks.

PREWRITING: Planning Your Research Paper

By this time, all of the information for your research paper should be on your note cards. Now it is time to plan your paper. Read over your notes and arrange them into separate stacks according to their content (for example, all cards on "History of Pyramids" in one pile, all cards on "Materials Used in Pyramids" in another). Then watch how your cards fall into a natural order of development.

The next step is to write a THESIS STATEMENT for your paper.

The THESIS STATEMENT expresses the main idea of a research paper.

Writing a Thesis Statement

Look back to page 37 and find the question you starred. This question is the basis for your thesis statement. For example, Joe chose the topic "Hurricanes." He asked the question, "What makes hurricanes so dangerous?" Joe wrote his thesis statement as follows:

> Hurricanes are one of the most destructive and unpredictable natural forces in the world, causing massive damage by both wind and water.

☑ Look again at your question on page 37. On a separate sheet of paper, rewrite your question in the form of a thesis statement as Joe did. When you have written your thesis statement, make sure that it matches the notes you have taken. You may find that your thesis statement doesn't quite fit the information you have found. If so, rewrite the statement so that it reflects your research.

48

Making an Outline

The outline, which is the skeleton of your research paper, must contain at least three MAIN TOPICS. These divisions are the broad categories that your notes fall into (the subject areas written at the top of your note cards). The main topics of an outline follow roman numerals and periods (I., II., III., IV.).

Each main topic may be divided into several SUBTOPICS. Subtopics contain more specific information about the subjects under which they're listed. Subtopics follow capital letters and periods (A., B., C.).

Subtopics can be further divided into SPECIFIC FACTS that follow arabic numerals (1., 2., 3., 4.). Each division (subtopics or specific facts) must contain at least two parts (A. and B. or 1. and 2.).

✓ Remember that the outline is the skeleton of a research paper. If parts of your outline aren't covered well in your notes, try to find more information. If you can't, omit those parts from your outline. Your outline and your paper should match each other exactly. Below is a sample outline to help you create your own.

Hurricanes

Thesis Statement: Hurricanes are one of the world's most destructive natural forces, causing massive damage by both wind and water.

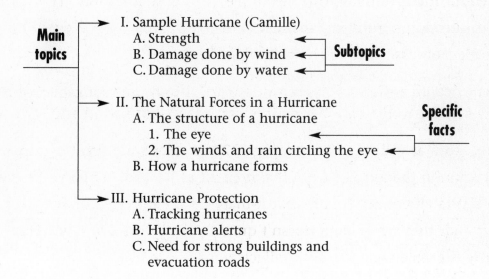

Main topics

I. Sample Hurricane (Camille)
   A. Strength
   B. Damage done by wind ← Subtopics
   C. Damage done by water

II. The Natural Forces in a Hurricane
   A. The structure of a hurricane
      1. The eye ← Specific facts
      2. The winds and rain circling the eye
   B. How a hurricane forms

III. Hurricane Protection
   A. Tracking hurricanes
   B. Hurricane alerts
   C. Need for strong buildings and
      evacuation roads

DRAFTING: Writing the First Draft

With your outline in hand and your notes beside it, you are almost ready to write the first draft of your research paper. Before you begin, however, use the checklist below to make sure you have all the information you will need.

	Yes	No
Topic		
Is appropriate (not too broad or too narrow)	✓	
Note Cards		
Contain enough information to write paper		
Each contains the author's name		
Each contains specific page numbers		
Notes are in your own words		
Quotations are properly punctuated		
Bibliography Cards		
A separate card for each source used		
Each card contains author's name (if known)		
Each card contains title of source		
Each card contains publisher, place, and date of publication		
Cards for magazines and reference books contain volume numbers and page numbers		
Outline		
Thesis statement written at top		
Contains at least three main topics		
Other subdivisions contain at least two sections		

If there are any checks in the No column, take time now to complete the missing information. You'll want to have all the information at your fingertips.

The outline you have made is like a road map. Use it to lead you through the development of your paper from beginning to end. Also be aware that a research paper contains the same parts as other papers you've written: an introduction, a body, and a conclusion.

Writing the Body

You may wonder why you are writing the body of the research report first. That is because writing the introduction and conclusion last saves you time. As you work on the body of your report—the main points you want to make—you will be thinking of your topic. By the time you finish, you will be able to take those thoughts and quickly introduce what you want to say. You won't leave anything out, and you will more closely show what you will be writing about.

The body of the paper is the largest section of your report and will contain most of the information you gathered. This part of your paper should come directly from your outline, following the same order. Sometimes a writer finds she must change her outline. She may find that the divisions of her outline don't work in the order in which she wrote them, or that she needs more information. She may decide she has new and better ideas for subtopics. If that should happen to you, change your outline.

Every paragraph in the body of your paper should be about a single idea. The *topic sentence* should state the main idea in the paragraph. Most often, you will want to write the topic sentence to begin the paragraph. The rest of the paragraph should be sentences that give facts and details about the topic sentence.

Here is the opening paragraph that Joe wrote for one of his subtopics, "The structure of a hurricane." Look back at page 49 and find the subtopic and specific facts he turned into words and sentences.

A hurricane is a giant whirling thundercloud surrounding an open center called the "eye." The eye of a hurricane is calm, but the winds that spiral around it are ferocious. Hurricanes have been clocked at up to 200 miles an hour.

You may find as you are writing that you need to do more research. Many writers find they can write a better report if they go back and do more research or rework their outline.

Here are some things to keep in mind as you begin to write the body of your report.

• *Place your stack of note cards in front of you in the order in which you will use them.* The information you will include in your report will come right from these cards. Everything should be in the order in which you need it. That way, you can keep writing instead of having to search for the right card.

• *Double-space your writing.* If you are writing your report by hand, skip lines to have room to make editing changes. If you are writing on a computer, you will want to print your double-spaced report so you can edit it more easily.

• *Use standard language.* You will sound like you know what you're talking about if you avoid slang. For example, don't say, "Another really cool thing about hurricanes is..."

• *Use few exclamation marks.* Save exclamation marks for informal or creative writing.

• *Understand you do not need a new sentence for each fact.* Sometimes you might want to combine facts in a sentence to make a sentence read more smoothly.

Now you are ready to write! Remember, this is a first draft. Expect that you will have changes to make both on your outline and in what you write.

DRAFTING: Writing the Introduction and Conclusion

The hardest part of the writing job is behind you. Now you can write the introduction and conclusion based on what you have already written.

The Introduction

The introduction you write has two jobs: it gets the reader's attention and previews the content of the paper. An introduction may be one or more paragraphs.

Here are the beginnings of three introductions for Joe's paper on hurricanes.

1. My paper will discuss the dangerous characteristics of hurricanes.

2. Hurricanes are one of nature's most powerful and uncontrollable forces.

3. A swirling storm, hundreds of miles wide, smashes docks and houses into toothpicks. It is a hurricane, one of nature's most destructive forces.

Which of the introductions above include part of Joe's thesis statement from page 49? Put a check mark beside the one that catches the reader's attention most effectively. Which introduction do you like the best?

There are many ways to introduce a report that will make the reader want to keep reading. Here are a few.

The Description

Joe's third introduction offers a description of a hurricane that makes a reader want to read on. It also tells what his report will be about—that hurricanes are one of the most destructive forces in the world. This is a good example of how to begin a research report with a description.

The Question

One good way to begin a research report is to begin with a question that intrigues your reader. He will read on to find the answer. For example, Joe might have begun his report this way:

What is one of the most destructive forces in the world, a force that can break boats apart, destroy buildings, and cause billions of dollars of damage?

The Quotation

You may have a great quotation in which someone makes a statement that can't help but interest the reader. Here is a sample Joe might have used:

"I don't know," said Jebert Hall, looking over what once was his house. "It's almost as if some giant reached right down and crushed this town in his fingers."

The Startling Fact

Sometimes in your research, you may run across a fact or statistic that fascinates you. If you feel that way, your reader may, too. Here is an example that might have begun Joe's report:

In 1992, a hurricane hit Florida. When it was all over, there was $12 billion in damage, thousands of people left homeless, and 50 people dead. Hurricanes are one of the most devastating and feared of natural forces.

You can use one of these approaches, or a different one. As you write, imagine you are the reader. Make sure you would want to keep reading the introduction you are writing. Now write the introduction to your research paper.

The Conclusion

The conclusion is the final part of your paper. This is the section where you can tell the reader what you have learned and how you feel about it. Try to leave your readers with something to think about. You may want to challenge them to some kind of action or inspire them to do more research on your topic. That's up to you. Remember, though, that a good conclusion will cause your reader to react in some way. Here is the conclusion Joe wrote:

> Scientists can't stop hurricanes or even predict their speed and direction. They can warn people who may be in the path of a deadly sea storm so that those who are threatened can take safety precautions. Knowing about hurricanes saves lives.

Joe went beyond his thesis statement to leave his reader something to think about. You can do that in your conclusion, too. You can also offer an opinion based on the research you did and the conclusions you reached from your research

If you don't want to go beyond your thesis statement, that's fine, too. If you restate your thesis statement and make your argument in a new way, that can be an effective conclusion.

Now write the conclusion to your research paper.

Compiling a Bibliography

REVISING: Improving Your Research Paper

Congratulations! You have completed the first draft of your research paper. Now it is time to check over your draft for ways to improve it.

Does your paper follow your outline exactly? If not, change either the outline or the paper so that they have the same order of development. Don't make a new copy of your paper unless it becomes too messy for you to read. Remember to cut and paste and to use proofreading marks.

Use this checklist to help you revise your report. Go over each point. If the item needs work, mark "Needs Work." Make the changes you need to make to improve your paper. Then mark the "Yes" column.

What You Need to Check:	Needs Work	Yes
Introduction:		
The opening gets the reader's attention.		
The introduction tells the reader what my report is about.		
Body:		
All the paragraphs in the report help support and prove the thesis statement.		
The ideas in the report follow the outline.		
Each paragraph has a topic sentence.		
Each paragraph has facts to support it.		
Conclusion:		
The conclusion tells the reader what I learned.		
The conclusion leaves the reader with something to think about.		

Transition Words

If all of the *content* of your paper seems satisfactory, it is time to check the way you wrote it. One way to improve your writing is by using TRANSITION WORDS to help your thoughts flow more smoothly.

TRANSITION WORDS connect one sentence to another or one paragraph to another.

The purpose of a transition word is to allow the reader to move smoothly from one idea to another. Read the paragraph below.

> The Spanish ship *Atocha* left Cuba in 1622. It was carrying gold, silver, and emeralds. The ship was brand new. It was poorly built. The *Atocha* sank in a storm. Its treasure rested on the bottom of the sea. It was found in 1985.

Did you notice that the sentences are short and choppy? One way to improve them is by adding transition words. Read the following revision. Why is this paragraph easier to read than the first one?

> When the Spanish ship *Atocha* left Cuba in 1622, it was carrying gold, silver, and emeralds. The ship was brand new, but it was poorly built. After the *Atocha* sank in a storm, its treasure rested at the bottom of the sea until it was found in 1985.

Circle words that are found in the second paragraph but not in the first. These words are called TRANSITION WORDS. They help the writer make a transition (move smoothly) from one statement or idea to the next. Some transition words and phrases are listed on the next page.

after	below	because	like
before	in	in spite of	as a result
finally	beside	therefore	for example
soon	although	but	in addition
next	next	near	however

Fill in the blanks below with words chosen from the lists above.

_____ it is 5000 years old, the Great Pyramid is still an

awe-inspiring sight. _____ , it is not as beautiful as it once must

have been. _____ its white limestone covering was gradually

stripped away to be used for other buildings, the pyramid is now a drab brown color.

_____, the temples that once surrounded it have been reduced

to rubble.

☑ Now that you are aware of the important role that transition words play in
making ideas flow easily from one to the other, read over your own paper. Add
transition words or phrases if needed.

REVISING: Using a Consistent Point of View

The following paragraph contains an error that is often made by beginning writers. Can you find it?

Halley's Comet returned in 1985 after a seventy-six-year absence. It looked like a glowing fuzzball in the winter sky. You could see it best in a dark area, away from city lights.

Because the paragraph is *grammatically* correct, the mistake may be hard to find. Read the information below and then try again.

Using Third Person Subjects

Research papers usually are written with third person subjects. Remember that there are three different "points of view" in writing:

FIRST PERSON: The writer speaks from his or her own point of view, as in "*I* read the book."

SECOND PERSON: The writer speaks about someone or something else, as in "*You* should read this book."

THIRD PERSON: The writer speaks about someone or something else, as in "*He* needs to read this book."

You have probably written your research paper from the third person point of view. Perhaps you have sometimes used the pronoun *it* or *they* as a sentence subject. Here is a rule to remember:

Use the third person of view throughout your research paper. Don't use *I* or *you* as a sentence subject in a research paper.

☑ Now find and correct the error (using proofreading marks) in the paragraph at the top of this page. Then check your research paper to be sure you have used the third person point of view consistently.

An important requirement for acknowledging borrowed material in a research paper is called a BIBLIOGRAPHY. It is an alphabetical list of all the sources you used as you researched your paper. When you compile a bibliography, you must use an exact, consistent form. Examples of different types of bibliographical entries follow.

Books

Author	Title (underlined)	City of Publication	Publisher	Date
Jones, John.	How to Track a Hurricane.	New York:	Templeton Press,	1961.

Magazines and other periodicals

Author	Title of Article	Magazine Title,	Vol.	Date	Page
Kluger, J.	"High Over the Eye."	Time	148,	September 16, 1996,	pages 70–71.

Title of Article	Title of Magazine	Date	Pages
"Hurricane Hullabaloo!"	Scientific American,	October 1996,	pages 34–35.

Author	Title of Article	Newspaper	Date	Page
Sawyer, Jane.	"Hurricane Strikes City."	Miami Post,	August 8, 1992,	page 1.

Encyclopedias and other reference books

Title of Article	Title of Reference Book	Vol.	Pages
"Hurricanes."	Universal Encyclopedia,	X,	pages 90–98.

Author	Title of Article	Title of Reference Book	Vol.	Pages
Smith, Ann	"Meteorology."	Youth Encyclopedia,	XII,	pages 160–164.

The samples above are divided into books, magazines, and encyclopedias to show you how each entry is made. Notice the following:

1. The third entry above does not include an author. If your article does not mention an author, list it alphabetically by the first letter in the first word of the title (excluding a, and, or the). If the author is listed, the entry should begin with his or her name, last name first.

2. If an entry is longer than one line, later lines are indented about five spaces inside the first line.

When you write your own bibliography, you will not divide the sources into books, magazines, and encyclopedias. You will simply list each entry in alphabetical order (using the author's name or, if none is given, the first word of the title). Be sure to punctuate and indent as shown below and to double-space your entries.

Here are the first two items as they would actually appear in the "Hurricane" bibliography. For practice, add the third and fourth items on the lines below.

"Hurricane Hullabaloo!" <u>Scientific American</u>, October 1996, pages 34–35.

"Hurricanes." <u>Universal Encyclopedia</u>, Vol. X, pages 90–98.

_____

_____

_____

_____

_____

_____

_____

_____

_____

_____

_____

_____

☑ Now prepare your own bibliography page. Where will you find the information? On your bibliography cards, of course! Arrange your cards in alphabetical order, using the rules above. Then use the examples on page 60 to get the information in the proper form and order.

PROOFREADING/PUBLISHING:
Preparing the Final Copy

Writing a Title

Before you make your final copy, you'll want to write an eye-catching title.
Here are the titles that Joe considered:

      1. Hurricanes   2. Weather Disasters

      3. Hurricanes: Great Storms from the Sea

Circle the title you think he should choose and explain your reasons:

_____

A good title attracts the attention of the reader and gives clues about the content of the paper.

Write three possible titles for your paper on the following lines.

1. _____

2. _____

3. _____

Review your titles carefully. Choose the one that you like most and rewrite it to make it more specific and interesting. Write your new title below.

_____

The Finishing Touches

✓ Use this checklist to be sure that you have completed all the steps of this long, challenging project. Pat yourself on the back for a job well done.

Topic

My topic is not too broad or too narrow. _____

My subject is appropriate for a research paper. _____

Source List

My list contains at least five sources. _____

My entries contain proper information. _____

Note Cards

Each card contains author's name and page number. _____

Each card contains one main idea. _____

Except for quotes, notes are written in my own words. _____

I punctuated my quotes properly. _____

Bibliography Cards

I filled out a card for each source I used. _____

Each card contains required information. _____

Outline

My outline begins with my thesis statement. _____

The outline contains at least three main topics. _____

I numbered and lettered topics and subtopics properly. _____

Final Paper

The content of my paper is complete and the writing interesting. _____

My paper follows the exact order of the outline. _____

I wrote the bibliography page correctly. _____

Mechanics

I have used correct capitalization, punctuation, and spelling. _____

My paper uses point of view correctly. _____

WRITING TO A PROMPT

What Is Writing to a Prompt?

Sometimes you get to choose what to write about. When someone else tells you what to write about, you are writing to a prompt. If your mother tells you to write a thank-you letter to your friend for a birthday present, that is writing to a prompt. If you sit down to take a test and the instructions say, "Explain which season you like best, and why," that is writing to a prompt, too.

A PROMPT is a topic you are asked to write about.

A prompt might ask you to write one of several different types of essays, including the following:

A Narrative Essay

A narrative tells a story. It may be either fiction (a short story with made-up characters) or nonfiction (for instance, the story of when you got lost in a park). When you are writing a narrative, you include a beginning, middle, and end, and usually you tell the story in the order in which the events happened.

An Expository Essay

Expository is another word for explaining. In an expository essay, you may be asked to give information about something, for example: "Tell about an animal you like, and why." You may be asked to explain something, for example: "Tell what you favorite sport is, and why."

A Descriptive Essay

In a *descriptive essay*, you describe a thing, person, event, or place, such as a room in your home or a blizzard. You write to appeal to your reader's senses. You try to make him see the place or thing—and sometimes to hear, smell, taste, and touch it as well.

A Persuasive Essay

To persuade is to try to convince someone to agree with you. A prompt for a persuasive essay might ask, "Should limits be placed on the amount of television children are allowed to watch?" Your job is to decide your point of view—what your opinion is. Then write arguments to persuade your reader to share your point of view.

How to Tell the Kind of Prompt

When you are asked to write to a prompt, the first thing to do is read the prompt carefully and decide what kind of essay the prompt is asking you to write. Is it narrative, expository, descriptive, or persuasive? Knowing the kind of essay will help you do a better job of planning and writing the essay.

When the Prompt Tells You Directly

Sometimes the prompt tells you exactly what kind of writing to do. For example:

Think back to a time when you were surprised. What surprised you?

Where were you? What were you doing? Who else was there? What did you think, say, and do? Write an essay in which you tell the story of this surprise.

If you read that prompt carefully, you know exactly what you should write: "tell the story" indicates a narrative essay.

Read for Clue Words

Sometimes the prompt doesn't tell you exactly what kind of writing to do. When this happens, look for clue words in the prompt, such as:

NARRATIVE

Narrate . . .

Tell a story about . . .

Write about a time . . .

What happened when . . .

EXPOSITORY

Explain . . .

Tell why . . .

Talk about . . .

Write why . . .

PERSUASIVE

Should there be . . .

Convince your reader that . . .

Support your view that . . .

Persuade your readers that . . .

Take a stand about . . .

Make an argument that . . .

What is your opinion . . .

DESCRIPTIVE

Describe . . .

Tell about an object . . .

What does it look and feel like . . .

Write so your reader can see . . .

Picture in your mind . . .

Prompts Without Clues

Not all prompts use those words, but most do. Sometimes, however, when there are no clue words, you have to figure out what kind of writing to do. For instance, read this prompt.

Write an essay about your favorite game.

How would you decide what kind of writing the prompt is asking for? One way is to ask yourself questions.

- Is this prompt asking for a description?
- Is this prompt asking for a story?
- Is this prompt asking for a persuasive essay?
- Is this prompt asking for an explanation?

Here is how one student thought about the prompt above: "I don't see any of the words that tell me right away what kind of writing to do. The prompt doesn't ask for any kind of story or experience, so it isn't narrative. It doesn't ask for an opinion, so it isn't persuasive. Descriptive essays focus on the way something looks, smells, feels, or sounds like, so it isn't asking for just a description. The prompt asks for an essay *about* a game, so it must be asking for an expository essay—writing that tells about or explains a game."

Of course, in explaining her favorite game, this student will include some descriptions as well. One kind of writing sometimes overlaps with another.

Which Type?

Here is an exercise that will give you practice in deciding what kind of essay to write in response to a prompt. Write *narrative, persuasive, expository,* or *descriptive* on each line below. Base your answers on the clue words you read, or, if you can't find any clue words, on what you think the prompt is asking for.

1. Everyone has a favorite possession. Tell what your favorite possession is and why it is important to you.

_____

2. Everyone has good days and bad days. Write a story about the best day you ever had.

_____

3. Imagine your family is planning a trip. You can visit anywhere in the world. Think of where you would like to go, and why. Write an essay that would convince your family to go to the place you choose.

_____

4. A person you know is planning to move to your town. She has written to you to ask you what it is like. Write a description of your town for her.

_____

5. Your parents are trying to decide whether to get a pet. Think if you would like to have a pet, and if so, what pet you would like. Then write an essay to persuade your family of your opinion.

_____

6. Think about your favorite food. In an essay, give reasons for liking this food best.

_____

The Steps of Writing to a Prompt

In this lesson, you will meet a student named Polly, who takes a test that asks her to write to a prompt. As you read what Polly does, notice the steps she goes through:

1. She decides what kind of writing the prompt is asking for.
2. She thinks of what she wants to say, and plans her writing.
3. She writes her first draft.
4. She revises her writing.
5. She proofreads her writing and corrects any errors in grammar, punctuation, and spelling.

Here is what Polly read when she opened the writing test booklet.

> When some people have free time, they like to ride their bikes. Others head for the computer to play a game, or walk to a friend's house to play. When you have free time, what do you like to do most? Tell what your favorite thing is to do when you have free time, and why it is your favorite thing.

Polly thought: *First, I need to decide what kind of writing to do. Are there any clue words in this writing prompt? I see the word "tell." I don't see any words like "describe," "convince," or "tell a story." I think this is asking me to explain, so I'll write an expository essay.*

Polly thought about what she liked to do when she had extra time. She liked to read, to play with her friends, and she especially liked to bake. She decided first to do some *prewriting*—to write quickly, just to get lots of ideas on paper. She decided to make a web. She wrote the word *baking* in a circle in the middle of a page. Then she thought of reasons she liked to bake, and what she liked to bake. She connected those ideas to the main idea, like this.

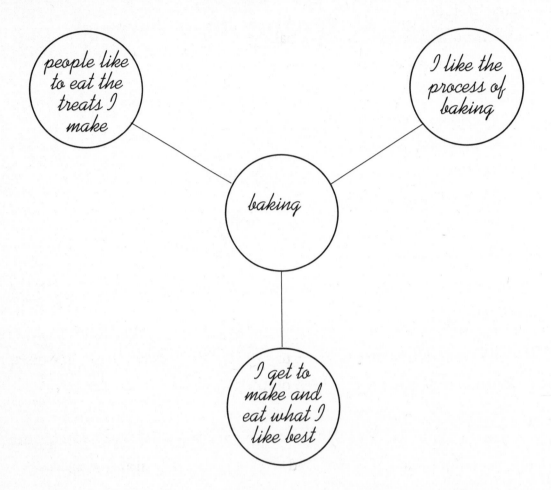

With her web finished, Polly could make a plan for writing. She knew she needed to include these things in her essay:

- An introduction that tells what she will be writing about
- At least three paragraphs in the body to tell the main points of the essay. Each paragraph should have a topic sentence and supporting details.
- A strong conclusion to tie up the essay's ideas and bring it to a satisfying close

Polly made a quick five-paragraph outline, with notes under each point about details she could include:

1. Introduction—My favorite thing is baking.
2. The process—what I do when I bake.

    cookbook

    flour, sugar, chocolate!

3. Everyone likes what I bake.

    chocolate chip cookies, brownies, fudge cakes

4. I get to eat my favorite things.

    brownies, cookies, cakes, blueberry muffins!

5. Conclusion

Practice Prewriting

Here is a prompt. Decide what kind of writing you need to do, and then use the space below to think about what you want to say. Use a web if you wish, and then write a quick outline in the space provided on the next page.

Imagine that you can have lunch with anyone alive today. Decide the person you would like to be with and write an essay explaining why you chose this person.

_____

_____

_____

_____

_____

_____

_____

_____

_____

_____

The First Draft

Let's look back at Polly's essay. With her outline to guide her, Polly wrote this first draft. She skipped a space between each line to leave room to make changes and corrections.

The minite I have some free time, I run to the kitchen to bake. Its my favorite thing to do when I have free time. I like all kinds of cooking, but baking is my favorite. I love everything about it from putting the ingredents together to watching my family eat what I make.

The first thing I lov about baking is the process, I love getting out the recipe book and reading the different recipes and picking out one to cook. I like getting the flour and eggs and chocolate (I love chocolate!) and setting them all out. Here are the things I like to make chocolate chip cookies chocolate cake chocolate pudding. Can you tell I like chcocolate. I like to make bread too, because my family likes to eat fresh bread for dinner.

I also really like to bake because everyone in my family likes it when I bake cookies, brownies an cakes. They say Polly, what smells so good? I tell them its my brownines. Do you want some? They say yes, Polly! And then everyone eats and likes my food I made, which makes me want to do it more. So I like to make good things to eat.

I like to bake to because when I bak I get to eat it. When you are the baker you get to chose what to make and I chose things I want to eat like brownies and cakes and blueberry muffins. I like to smell them when they cook and think about eating a warm muffin. Especially because I know I made it!

Everybody liks when I bake and I do to!

The Second Draft

When Polly looked at her work, she wasn't satisfied. She knew she could do better. She decided to revise.

Here is her revised draft.

The minute I have some free time, I run to the kitchen to bake. It's my favorite thing to do in my spare time. Although I like all kinds of cooking, baking is my favorite. I love everything about it, from putting the ingredients together, to watching my family enjoy what I bake, to having them beg me to bake something else.

The first thing I love about baking is the process. I love getting out the recipe book and reading about all the delicious cakes, cookies, and other desserts. I love pulling out the big bag of white flour—it always gets all over me! I like taking the cool, smooth eggs from the refrigerator. I love the squares of chocolate in their silver wrappers. I like to set out everything that I will be using, and then measure and mix and turn on the oven and set the timer. Doing all that organizing makes me feel like a professional baker.

I also really like to bake because everyone in my family enjoys what I bake. Most of all they like my chocolate deserts, such as chocolate chip cookies, fudge cake, and chocolate pudding. When the sweet smell starts to fill the house, everyone asks, "Polly, what smells so good?" When I tell them it's my special brownies, they smile and take a big sniff and rub their hands together. That just makes me want to bake more!

Finally, I have a secret: I like to bake to because I get to eat what I make. I love to think about eating a warm cookie, with the chocolate chips all melted and gooey when I put the cookie in my mouth. My other favorite is a hot blueberry muffin, right out of the oven, especially on a cold winter morning.

I know other people like to make models, or play basketball, or knit. For me, though, no hobby is as fun as baking. I get to do everything myself. I get to hear my family tell me how great I am. You can't eat a basketball, but you sure can eat a warm chocolate chip cookie!

How Did Polly Do?

Remember, Polly wrote her essay for a test. Her writing will receive a score. The scorers will be looking for certain things. They might use a checklist like the one on the next page.

LESSON 2

Rate the essay from 1 (lowest) to 4 (highest) on each of the following

Organization The essay has an introduction, body, and conclusion. The essay proceeds smoothly from point to point. The writer uses transitions when necessary.		
Focus The subject is clear, and the writer stays on subject. All paragraphs and sentences relate to the subject of the essay. Each paragraph has a main idea and supporting details.		
Language Sentences are interesting and varied. The writer uses specific, well-chosen details. Words are vivid, strong, and used correctly.		
Conventions Sentences are complete. Grammar is correct. Punctuation and capitalization are correct. Spelling is correct.		

Writing to a Narrative Prompt

Do you remember what a *narrative* prompt asks you to do?

A narrative prompt asks you to tell a story. The prompt might tell you if the story should be real or made up.

If a prompt asks you to write a narrative, here are the main points to keep in mind.

Organize Your Narrative

Persuasive, expository, and descriptive essays are all organized around ideas, or main points. But narrative writing tells a story, and that means you should use a different kind of organization. In general, narrative writing moves in chronological order, telling the events that happened from first to last.

In an expository essay, you would probably announce the topic of each paragraph in a topic sentence. For a narrative, your paragraphs do not need to have a topic sentence. Each paragraph, however, should focus on a single event, with all the sentences in the paragraph about that event. Each step of the story should be clear, with one event leading to the next, one paragraph at a time.

Include Good Details and Descriptions

Precise details and descriptions are important in any kind of writing, and that goes for narrative writing, too. Make sure to describe how people, places, and things look, smell, act, and feel. Try to make your reader see "a movie in his mind." You want to show, not tell, your reader what happened. You can best do that by offering precise details and descriptions. For example:

Telling: He was a hard worker.
Showing: His muscles bulged and the sweat poured from his forehead as he shoveled load after load of dirt.

Include Dialogue, if Possible

Compare these two passages:

The announcer said that I had won the award.

The announcer opened the envelope, looked at the card, and said in a loud voice, "And the award goes to Brett Johnson!"

Which way better *shows* your reader what happened? By using dialogue, the second sentence puts your reader into the action. It lets him *hear* what was said.

Writing to a Narrative Prompt

Follow these steps to write to a narrative prompt.

1. **Identify the prompt as narrative.** Here's a reminder of the guidelines for figuring out if the prompt is asking for a narrative:
   - You see the clue words *narrative, story, tell about a time,* or *tell what happened.* Those words tell you that the prompt is asking for a narrative.
   - If there are no clue words, ask yourself if the best response to the prompt would be a story, a description, a persuasive argument, or an essay that explains something. If the best response is to tell a story with a beginning, middle, and end, write a narrative.

Read these two prompts. Write *narrative* in front of the narrative prompt.

   narrative Think back to when you had a happy experience. Remember where you were and what happened. Were you alone or with someone else? When did this happen? What were your thoughts at the time, and what did people say? How did you feel? Write a story about that happy experience.

_____ Everyone has a place he or she likes best. Write about your favorite place, describing what you like about it, where it is, and when you go there. Write so that your reader can see, feel, smell, and hear the place.

2. **Plan your writing.** You will be writing to the prompt that asks you to write a story about a time when you felt happy. Remember that your story needs characters, a setting, and a plot. Write each of those words on a sheet of scratch paper, and then freewrite to think of ideas. For example:

characters	setting	plot
Coach Wilson	baseball field	Championship game.
my parents	locker room	Coach put me in to pinch-hit!
Bobby (pitcher)	restaurant (after game)	Oh no—two strikes.
me!		Swing—a hit!
		Celebration after game.

To organize your essay, make a plan that lists the events in the order in which they happened. You can make a diagram like the one you used in Unit 1 for your memoir, which is a kind of narrative. Be sure to include details, and try to note where dialogue would work well.

First event: _____
detail _____
detail _____

Second event: _____
detail _____
detail _____

Third event: _____
detail _____
detail _____

Fourth event: _____
detail _____
detail _____

Either write a plan in the space below, or use a separate sheet to make a diagram like the one on the previous page.

The day and weeks leading up
to Malachi beeing born.

Now that you have made a plan, it's time to write your draft. (Follow the directions on the next page.)

3. Write a first draft. Just as in the other writing you do, writing a first draft can help you get out your ideas. After that, you can revise. If you look at Polly's efforts, you can see that in her first draft, she did not worry too much about spelling or grammar. She knew she could work on those later.

On a separate sheet of paper, write your first draft. Follow your plan as you write. Write on every other line so that you have room to revise what you write. Here is the prompt again:

> Think back to when you had a happy experience and remember where you were and what happened. Were you alone or with someone else? When did this happen? What were your thoughts at the time, and what did people say? How did you feel? Write a story about that happy experience.

4. Revise your work. In this step, you take a hard look at what you wrote, think of ways to improve it, and then revise. Ask yourself these questions, and if your writing needs work, revise it:

- Does your introduction tell what you will be writing about and interest your reader?
- Does your body develop the story, with each paragraph telling about a different event?
- Does your conclusion include the ending of your story, and perhaps tell what it meant to you?

5. Proofread your work. The last step is looking at your revised work to make sure no errors have crept in. Pay particular attention to spelling, grammar, punctuation, and capitalization. When you have examined every sentence and made all corrections, you are finished.

How Did You Do?

Here is a checklist that scorers might use to evaluate a narrative essay.

Rate the essay from 1 (lowest) to 4 (highest) on each of the following

Organization The essay has an introduction, body, and conclusion. The essay proceeds smoothly from point to point. The writer uses transitions when necessary.	
Focus The subject is clear, and the writer stays on subject. All paragraphs and sentences relate to the subject of the essay. Each paragraph has a main idea and supporting details.	
Language Sentences are interesting and varied. The writer uses specific, well-chosen details. Words are vivid, strong, and used correctly.	
Conventions Sentences are complete. Grammar is correct. Punctuation and capitalization are correct. Spelling is correct.	

Writing to an Expository Prompt

In some ways, writing an expository essay is like writing a narrative. In both, you make your writing as well-organized and clear as you can; you have a beginning, middle, and end; you stick to the topic; and, you make sure the conventions (grammar, spelling, punctuation, capitalization) are correct. In expository writing, though, you approach some things differently.

The Purpose of an Expository Essay

A narrative essay tells a story, but an expository essay instructs, gives information, or explains. You aren't trying to persuade someone or make him believe you are right—that's what you do in a persuasive essay. You aren't trying simply to describe—that's a descriptive essay.

Here are examples of prompts for expository essays:

- Explain why a person in your life is special.
- What one thing would you change to make this country a better place to live?
- What book that you have read have you liked the most, and why?

Developing Paragraphs

In a narrative essay, each paragraph develops an event in a story. But in an expository essay, each paragraph focuses on a single idea, supported by details.

In an expository essay, most paragraphs have three parts:

1. The topic sentence
2. The body (details and supporting information)
3. The closing sentence

The Topic Sentence

In an expository essay, every paragraph should have a main idea, which you should state in a topic sentence. The topic sentence announces the main idea of the paragraph, or what the paragraph is going to be about. Especially when writing for a prompt, it is a good idea to write the topic sentence as the first sentence of the paragraph.

The Body

The sentences that follow the topic sentence make up the body of the paragraph. These sentences give information and add details to support the topic. All of the sentences should support and relate directly to the topic sentence.

The Closing Sentence

In some paragraphs, the last sentence works as a closing sentence. A closing sentence wraps up a paragraph by emphasizing the main idea that was announced in the topic sentence. A closing sentence is often an echo or a reflection of the opening sentence. The closing sentence should be the thought or idea that you want the reader to remember most.

Read this paragraph from an expository essay written in response to this prompt: "Explain why a person in your life is special."

Most of all, my grandmother is wise. She can look at me and see instantly that I have something on my mind I need to talk about. She knows when not to talk to me, too. She has a huge supply of stories and sayings on just about every topic, from the importance of saving, to the sadness of having a fight with a friend. More than just being smart, my grandmother is truly wise.

Now read the paragraph again, and this time identify the topic sentence, the body, and the closing sentence.

Write to an Expository Prompt

Follow these steps to write to an expository prompt.

1. Decide if you should write an expository essay.

When you are reading a prompt, look for key words such as "tell about" and "explain" that mean you should write an expository essay. If you don't see key words, decide if the prompt is *mostly* asking for

- An opinion you want to persuade someone about
- A story
- A description
- An explanation

If you will be writing an explanation, or telling about something, you are writing an expository essay, even if you will be doing some describing, or telling your opinion.

Which of the following prompts asks you to write an expository essay? Write *expository* in the blank in front of the expository prompt.

_____Everyone has wanted to be a hero. Maybe you have been a hero. Tell about a time in which you were a hero, or write a story you make up in which you are the hero. Tell what happened, and what made you heroic.

_____What invention do you think has been the most important? Write about the invention that you think has made the most difference to the world. Tell why you think this invention is so important.

2. Plan your expository essay.

The prompt about the invention is asking for an expository essay. Think of which invention you want to write about. Now think about three or more main points you want to make, and what details will support each of these points. Fill in the web on the next page with that information.

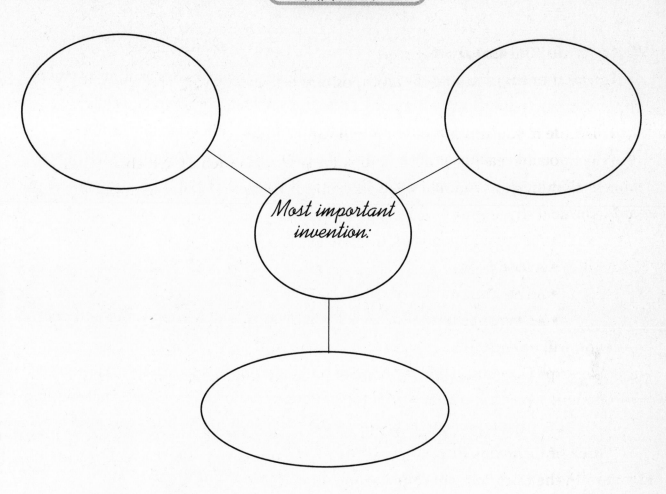

Most important invention:

3. Outline your essay.

Use the lines below to make a quick outline of what you want to write. Include your introduction, the body (which should have at least three main ideas), and the conclusion.

_____

_____

_____

_____

_____

_____

_____

4. Write your first draft.

Write your first draft on a separate sheet of paper. Follow your outline as you write. You may want to write the body of your essay first, and then add the introduction and conclusion. If you do that, you will be able to easily write the introduction and conclusion. Remember that you will be revising and proofreading your first draft. Write on every other line so that you have room to revise what you write.

5. Revise your essay.

Keep these points in mind as you revise your essay:

- Does your introduction tell what you will be writing about and grab your reader?
- Does your body develop each main point in a paragraph? Does each paragraph start with a topic sentence followed by details that support that topic sentence? Does each paragraph in the body end with a closing sentence?
- Does your conclusion wrap up what you want to say in a satisfying way?

6. Proofread your essay.

Make a clean final copy of your essay. Then check your paper to catch and correct any errors. Look carefully at spelling, punctuation, capitalization, and grammar.

How Did You Do?

Here is a checklist that scorers might use to evaluate an expository essay.

Rate the essay from 1 (lowest) to 4 (highest) on each of the following

Organization The essay has an introduction, body, and conclusion. The essay proceeds smoothly from point to point. The writer uses transitions when necessary.	
Focus The subject is clear, and the writer stays on subject. All paragraphs and sentences relate to the subject of the essay. Each paragraph has a main idea and supporting details. There is enough information to explain the topic.	
Language Sentences are interesting and varied. The writer uses specific, well-chosen details. Words are vivid, strong, and used correctly.	
Conventions Sentences are complete. Grammar is correct. Punctuation and capitalization are correct. Spelling is correct.	

Writing to a Descriptive Prompt

An expository essay or narrative may include some description, and many of the best do. For example, if you are writing a story, you will want to describe how characters look or what the setting is like. In a descriptive essay, however, the focus is almost entirely on description.

Here are two prompts for descriptive essays:

Imagine that you have to explain a season of the year to someone who lives in a place without that climate—for example, explain winter to someone who lives near the Equator. Choose the season you like best and describe it. You can use sights, sounds, smells, and the way things feel in your essay.

Everyone has a piece of clothing he or she treasures. It may be your most comfortable sweatshirt. It may be the coat you only wear for special occasions. It may be a pair of jeans that makes you remember a hike with a friend. Picture that piece of clothing in your mind. Now describe it for your reader so he or she will be able to picture it clearly. Tell how it looks and feels. You can also write about how it smells and the sound it makes when you move.

You might organize a descriptive essay about the piece of special clothing this way:

- Paragraph 1: an introduction that tells what the piece of clothing is and why it is important to you
- Paragraphs 2-4: one paragraph that explains what it feels like to wear it, another paragraph that explains what it looks like to you, and a

third paragraph that tells how your friends have described it

- Paragraph 5: an ending paragraph in which you summarize the descriptions of the piece of clothing

In a descriptive essay, a paragraph in the middle of the essay would contain a topic sentence that gives a description, and the other sentences would back up that description with details. Here is an example of a paragraph that might appear in an essay about a favorite jacket.

I know this jacket is old, and my mother wants me to get a new one, but I like it because it's old. It has leather elbows that are cracked and worn, with whitish cracks that look like a spider web in the leather. Its color was once a fire-engine red, but now it's closer to dusty rose. Its collars and cuffs are frayed, with little threads that I can feel on my neck and wrists. I think this jacket might be older than my mother!

Notice that this paragraph focuses on details about how old this jacket is. How does the writer help us *see* the old jacket? What adjectives does he use? Can you find a simile in the description?

Write to a Descriptive Prompt

Follow these steps to write to a descriptive prompt.

1. Decide if you should write a descriptive essay.

Look for key words such as "describe" and "tell how it looks, smells, and sounds." Those words tell you that you will be writing a descriptive essay.

Which of the following prompts asks you to write a descriptive essay? Write *descriptive* in the blank in front of the descriptive prompt.

_____ You may live in a town, a city, or the country. Describe the place where you live. Tells what it looks, sounds, smells, and feels like to live where you do.

_____ Imagine you want a pet, but that you need to convince your parents to let you have one. Write an essay in which you give reasons that would persuade your parents.

2. Plan your essay.

To write to the descriptive prompt, think of how you would describe where you live. Then think of three main points you could make. You might make a web with "Where I live" in the center bubble. In the three outer bubbles, write notes about how the place looks, sounds, and smells.

3. Write a quick outline.

Use your web to make an outline that has an introduction, at least three paragraphs for the body (you might use a paragraph for each sense—sight, sound, and smell), and a conclusion.

4. Write your first draft.

Write your first draft on a separate sheet of paper, following your outline.

5. Revise your essay.

Look at your introduction, body, and conclusion to make sure your essay is well-organized and that paragraphs in the body have a topic sentence, supporting sentences, and a closing sentence.

6. Proofread your essay.

Make a clean final copy of your essay, and then check your paper to catch and correct any errors.

How Did You Do?

Here is a checklist that scorers might use to evaluate a descriptive essay.

Rate the essay from 1 (lowest) to 4 (highest) on each of the following

Organization The essay has an introduction, body, and conclusion. Each paragraph adds something new to the description. The essay proceeds smoothly from point to point.	
Focus The subject is clear, and the writer stays on subject. All paragraphs and sentences relate to the subject of the essay. Each paragraph has a main idea and supporting details. The description gives a detailed picture of the subject of the essay.	
Language Sentences are interesting and varied. The writer uses specific, well-chosen details. Words are vivid, strong, and used correctly.	
Conventions Sentences are complete. Grammar is correct. Punctuation and capitalization are correct. Spelling is correct.	

Writing to a Persuasive Prompt

When you write a persuasive essay, you state an opinion and then try to convince your reader to share it. Persuasive writing is a kind of expository writing, and follows a similar structure:

- An introduction, in which you get the reader's attention and tell what you will be writing about
- A body, in which you develop three or more main points, each in a separate paragraph, with supporting details and a closing sentence
- A conclusion, in which you wrap up your topic and bring your essay to a satisfying close

Here are two prompts for a persuasive essay.

Some towns have curfew laws that say children under the age of 18 must be inside their homes by midnight. Are you for or against a curfew? Decide how you feel, then make your arguments in an essay.

Some people think that television is bad for children. Should children be allowed to watch television? Write an essay in which you make an argument for either side of this question.

An essay arguing that television is not bad for children might be organized this way:

- Paragraph 1: an introduction that explains the subject and tells what you will try to persuade the reader about in this essay
- Paragraphs 2-4: paragraphs that each give a reason for your belief, and sentences that support each reason, including a paragraph that deals with the other side of the argument

- Paragraph 5: a conclusion in which you wrap up your writing and leave your reader with your argument for allowing children to watch television

Seeing the Other Side

When you write a persuasive essay, it's a good idea to show that you are aware of the main arguments against your opinion. Don't try to attack those arguments. Just calmly state them, and then go on to show why your opinion is stronger. For example, an essay that says television is not bad for children might say something like this:

> Of course television can be bad for children in some ways. Watching too much television is not a good idea. Parents should limit the amount of television their children can watch, and encourage their children to read and do active things like sports. Parents also need to be sure that children don't watch shows that are bad for them. Gossip shows, violent crime shows, and cartoons with foul language are not good for children or anyone else.

That paragraph shows that the writer is a reasonable person who can understand why some people might think that television is bad for children. But then the writer might go on and write a paragraph like this:

> While television can be bad in some ways, it is good in many others. Television can be a way for children to learn things they could never learn otherwise. On television, a child can hear and see a great speech, such as the "I have a dream" speech of Martin Luther King, Jr. Thanks to television, a child can learn things about nature that he or she would never be able to see in person. A child who lives in downtown Los Angeles can visit the rain forest of South America. Through television, a child can learn about the world.

What is the topic of that paragraph? What details does the writer offer to support the topic?

Writing the Conclusion

The conclusion of a persuasive essay is your final chance to convince your reader. You can briefly restate your strongest reasons, and bring your reasons together in a strong, final sentence. Here is an example from the essay about children and television.

Television can be one of the best ways to help a child's world grow. Through television, children can sample great plays. They can visit the world and learn things they would never see in person. Television can help children keep up with current events. With supervision, the world of television can open the world to a child.

Write to a Persuasive Prompt

Follow these steps to write to a persuasive prompt.

1. Decide if you should write a persuasive essay.

Look for key words such as *convince, argument, opinion,* and *persuade.* Those words tell you that you will be writing a persuasive essay.

Which of the following prompts asks you to write a persuasive essay? Write *persuasive* in the blank in front of the persuasive prompt.

_____ Your family is planning a vacation. Think of the place you would most like to visit. Write an essay in which you convince your family to visit the place you want to go.

_____ Imagine your favorite toy from when you were younger has come to life. Write a story in which you tell about an adventure your toy had.

2. Plan your descriptive essay.

Use a web or list to help you plan where your family should visit.

3. Write a quick outline.

Use your plan to create an outline with an introduction, three paragraphs in the body, and a conclusion.

4. Write your first draft.

Write your essay, using the outline for guidance.

5. Revise your essay.

Look at how you organized your essay, and at each paragraph. Does each paragraph have a topic sentence? Do all sentences in the paragraph relate to the topic sentence?

6. Proofread your essay.

Make a clean copy and check to make sure it contains as few errors as possible. See the next page for a checklist.

How Did You Do?

Here is a checklist that scorers might use to evaluate a persuasive essay.

Rate the essay from 1 (lowest) to 4 (highest) on each of the following

Organization The essay has an introduction, body, and conclusion. The essay proceeds smoothly from point to point.	
Focus The subject is clear, and the writer stays on subject. All paragraphs and sentences relate to the subject of the essay. Each paragrpah lists a reason and details that support that reason. There is enough information to persuade the reader.	
Language Sentences are interesting and varied. The writer uses specific, well-chosen details. Words are vivid, strong, and used correctly.	
Conventions Sentences are complete. Grammar is correct. Punctuation and capitalization are correct. Spelling is correct.	

WRITING AN EDITORIAL

What Is an Editorial?

Imagine that you open a newspaper and see this headline for a news article:

CONSTRUCTION BEGINS ON NEW PARKWAY

The article tells where the new road is being built. It identifies the company building the road. It describes the speech the mayor gave at the ceremony to begin construction. It points out that nearby, a group of people carried signs with messages like, "Build homes, not roads!" and chanted, "No, no, the parkway has to go!"

The article reports the facts about the new parkway. The facts show that some people are in favor of the parkway and some are against it. Still, this article does not express an opinion on whether the parkway is a good or bad thing. That's the job of a news article—to report the facts and leave out the writer's opinions.

But a few pages later, you come across another article with this headline:

PARKWAY GOOD FOR AREA BUSINESSES

This article *does* express an opinion. The writer argues that the parkway is good because it will bring in more tourists and more business. He also says that it will provide jobs for people in the community. He says it will make the community safer because the parkway will allow big trucks to drive around the city instead of through it. The writer points out that even though the route of the parkway requires that five old homes be torn down, the city has paid the families so they can buy new homes. The writer concludes that the parkway is a real benefit for the community.

This article, in which the writer expresses an opinion on an issue, is called an *editorial*. Besides stating the writer's opinion, an editorial also gives facts and reasons to support that opinion.

An editorial is a kind of *persuasive essay*. (In the last unit, you learned about writing persuasively in response to a prompt.) When you write an editorial, you try to persuade your readers to agree with you and accept your ideas on an issue. The skills required to write a good editorial are important for any kind of persuasive writing.

Editorials are an important part of newspapers. You will find them on the editorial pages, also called the Op-Ed pages. Op-Ed is short for Opinion-Editorial.

Let's take a look at what you can find on the Op-Ed pages of most newspapers.

The Parts of the Editorial Pages

Look at the Op-Ed pages in your local newspaper. See if you can find each of the following items:

1. An editorial. An editorial usually is not signed with the writer's name. Often, you will find editorials on the left side of the editorial page. Write the headline of an editorial you find on the line below.

_____

2. Letters to the editor. These are the opinions of the newspaper's readers, usually in response to a story or editorial in the newspaper. Write the headline or first sentence of a letter to the editor on the line below.

_____

3. An editorial column. This is an article written by a journalist or writer who has a regular space to offer his or her thoughts and opinions on issues. Write the headline of a column on the editorial pages, as well as the name of the columnist, on the line below.

_____

4. An editorial cartoon. Instead of writing articles, cartoonists use drawings to express their opinion on issues. What opinion do you think this cartoonist is expressing?

_____

_____

The Parts of an Editorial

While editorials express very different opinions, many follow a similar pattern:

- *Introduction:* The first paragraph usually includes a statement of what the problem or issue is, and what the editorial writer's opinion is.
- *Body:* The middle paragraphs sometimes give the background information about the issue. Most of all, they give facts and reasons for the writer's opinion.
- *Conclusion:* The final paragraph often restates the writer's opinion and encourages readers to think in a different way or to take action.

Here is an editorial written by a student concerned about support for her community's animal shelter.

SUPPORT THE ANIMAL SHELTER
by Melissa Gant

The Have-a-Heart Animal Shelter is in trouble. Last month, the shelter's board of directors announced that the shelter might have to close unless more donations come in. Last week the Jefferson Area Youth Soccer League raised more than $5,000 for the shelter. This was a good start, but it is only a beginning. The shelter is important for our community, and we need to do more to make sure that it stays open.

The Have-a-Heart Shelter almost closed because it didn't have enough money. Volunteers work for free, but the shelter has to pay for the upkeep of the shelter, as well as food, medicine, and other supplies. According to the shelter's director, Dr. Frances Moore, food for one animal for a year costs about $300, and for every animal the shelter takes in, it must turn away another.

Our town needs the shelter. The shelter takes care of injured wild animals as well as giving homes to stray cats and dogs. Keeping the shelter open is important—according to Dr. Moore, the shelter takes care of more than 500 animals a year. Since there is no other shelter in the area, without the Have-a-Heart Shelter these animals would likely be destroyed.

Some people say that there are more important things to donate their money to. It's true, there are many good causes worthy of support, such as the Friends of the Library and the Jefferson Area Food Bank. But the way a community cares for its most helpless residents, animals as well as people, tells what that community is like. By raising money to help care for animals that have been abandoned, or are wild and injured, we show that we are a caring community.

To help raise money for the shelter, we should hold an "Animal Fair" every year, right next to the soccer fields. The fair could be held on the days of the tournament at the end of the soccer season, since so many people come to the tournament. This would be a good time to have bake sales, car washes,

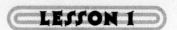

and raffles. We could sell tickets for an obstacle course. Children could have fun on the course as they pretend to be swinging monkeys or running cheetahs. The money we make could help support the shelter.

As people who care about animals and our community, it is our job to make sure the shelter stays open. It is the only place for stray animals to go, and the only place that will save them. Our community should be good to animals, and that means raising money to keep the Have-a-Heart Shelter open. We can show that we are a community that cares.

Analyze the editorial above by answering these questions.

1. What problem or issue is the writer addressing?

_____

_____

2. What is the writer's opinion on the issue?

_____

_____

3. What is one fact or reason the writer gives to support her opinion?

_____

_____

Prewriting: Choosing a Topic

We all have opinions. When you write an editorial, you have the chance to persuade others to share your opinions on an issue. To be convincing, you need to choose a topic that:

- You know about, or can find out about
- You have a strong opinion about
- Is narrow enough to be manageable
- You can research to find facts to back up your opinions.

Before you choose a topic, let's think about the difference between facts and opinions.

Facts and Opinions

A fact is something that is true. For example, "Cats have four legs"—that's a fact. An opinion is something you believe but that not everyone believes. For example, "Cats are better pets than dogs"—that's an opinion. Opinions are subject to disagreement, but facts are always true.

Practice telling fact from opinion by completing the exercise below. If a statement is an opinion, write **O**. If it is a fact, write **F**.

1. ____ Professional baseball has changed its rules over the years.
2. ____ Baseball is the best sport.
3. ____ Libraries need to provide more computers for public use.
4. ____ "The Star-Spangled Banner" is the national anthem of the United States.
5. ____ "The Star-Spangled Banner" is a beautiful song.
6. ____ Some state laws require that people on motorcycles wear helmets.
7. ____ Everyone should support the drive to collect used books for the sale.
8. ____ You should visit Paris once in your lifetime.
9. ____ The Internet is the greatest invention of all time.
10. ____ There are millions of websites on the Internet.

Choose a Suitable Topic

You may have opinions about many things, but not all are suitable topics for editorials. Here are guidelines to help you choose a topic that will work well.

1. You should be able to back up your topic with facts and expert opinions. Read this topic:

> Chocolate tastes better than vanilla.

That is a personal preference, and you can't use facts to back it up. People have different tastes, but personal preference by itself does not make a good topic for an editorial.

2. Choose a topic that is neither too broad nor too narrow. Think carefully about the topic you choose to make sure it is neither too broad to be able to cover in a single editorial, nor so narrow that there is little to say about the topic. Here are examples:

TOO BROAD: America is a strong country.

That topic is not only too broad, but too vague--think of all the ways you could interpret "strong."

TOO NARROW: The block between 1st and 2nd on Elm is cracking, and should be repaved.

You might be able to prove this with facts, but it is such a narrow topic that few people would be interested.

Read the topics below. Think whether they would make suitable topics for an editorial. After each write *suitable, too narrow, too broad,* or *personal preference.*

1. Skiers should be required to wear helmets.

2. Trees are good for the Earth.

_____

3. White is the best color for a house.

_____

4. Our community needs to build more playing fields for youth sports.

_____

5. A breakfast of oatmeal is best.

_____

6. Action movies are the most enjoyable kind of movies.

_____

7. This community should open a recycling center.

_____

8. The broken basketball hoop in Franklin Park should be fixed immediately.

_____

Finding Ideas for an Editorial

You may already have an opinion about an issue or problem you want to write about. If not, here are some ways to find topics:

- Look at the newspaper for ideas of events and ideas you care about.
- Talk to friends and family about important issues in your community and in the world.
- Watch a television current events show or newscast for ideas.
- Read a newsmagazine for topics that people are discussing.

One way to think of a topic for an editorial is to ask questions on which people disagree about the answers. For example: Should there be a law requiring all bicycle riders to wear helmets?

Try to add a question in each of the subject areas below.

Science:
Should the United States government spend money to send people to Mars?

_____

_____

Television:
Should advertising for junk food be banned?

_____

_____

Government:
Should cities have curfew laws that require young people to be off the streets before midnight?

_____

_____

Community Affairs:
Should our community support the building of a new parkway?

_____

_____

Keep in mind that the question itself is not the topic for an editorial. Instead, the topic is your answer to the question. When you answer the question, you take a stand, you express an opinion—and that's where an editorial begins.

The Thesis Statement

The sentence in which you write the problem and your opinion of the problem is your thesis statement. Reread Melissa's first paragraph below:

> The Have-a-Heart Animal Shelter is in trouble. Last month, the shelter's board of directors announced that the shelter might have to close unless more donations come in. Last week the Jefferson Area Youth Soccer League raised more than $5,000 for the shelter. This was a good start, but it is only a beginning. *The shelter is important for our community, and we need to do more to make sure that it stays open.*

The sentence in italics is Melissa's thesis statement. It tells the topic, and her opinion on the topic. Think about the thesis statement you wrote for your research paper. It directed all the writing you did. Your paper was organized to prove your thesis statement. The same is true in editorial writing. Your editorial proves your thesis statement.

Here are more examples of thesis statements for editorials:

> Bike helmets can save lives, so we need to pass a law to require that everyone riding a bike wear a helmet.

> Because junk food hurts kids' health, television stations should not allow junk food advertising on children's programs.

> Our community needs more soccer fields, and we should raise money to build them.

Freewriting Ideas

In the space below, write ideas for possible editorials. Write as much as you can. Don't stop writing because you think, "Oh, that won't work." Write down *all* the ideas you can think of.

_____

_____

_____

_____

_____

_____

_____

Look at your ideas and choose the one you like best. On the lines below, write a thesis statement based on that idea. Your thesis statement should include what the problem is and your opinion about it. Make sure you write it as a statement, not a question.

_____

_____

_____

Prewriting: Gathering Information and Taking Notes

It's fine to have an opinion, but to write an editorial about it you need more than just the way you feel. There is a big difference between having an opinion and having an *informed* opinion—an opinion backed by facts that can be proven to be true. Read the following statements. Which would you believe?

> I think Chinese is the most commonly spoken language in the world.

> Chinese, with 885 million speakers, is the most widely spoken language in the world.

The second statement, of course, is more persuasive. It is based on a fact, not a guess. To convince your reader, you need evidence—facts and information to support your opinion.

Finding the Evidence

You can find evidence to support your opinion in several places.

Personal Experience

You can use personal experience to back up your opinion. If you saw something happen, or if it happened to you, you can speak about it with authority. Imagine you are writing about the need for more soccer fields. You play soccer, and have had games cancelled because not enough fields were available. That is a fact you can use.

Knowledge from Experts

You may be able to talk to people who are experts, or who know the facts. For the editorial about the lack of soccer fields, you could interview the head of the parks department for your community. She might tell you that there is a waiting list of fifteen teams that want to schedule playing time. That is a fact you can use.

Someone who studies what you are writing about is an expert. For instance, if you were writing about an endangered animal, you might want to talk to a biology professor.

If you need to find an expert with information, try:

- Asking people who know about your topic whom they respect and go to for information
- Checking to see if you can find officials and others who are quoted or used as sources in local news articles

Conducting an Interview

Here are some tips for interviewing people.

1. Have your questions ready. Think about what you want to find out, and write a list of questions before you meet with the person.
2. Write down exact answers to your questions. In general, you can write brief notes instead of full sentences. But if you think you might quote the person you are interviewing, be careful to write down his exact words. It's a good idea to read what you have written back to the person you're interviewing so he can make sure you got it right.
3. Make sure you understand what the person is telling you. If you don't, ask him or her to explain the information again.
4. Ask if you can call back if you need more help. Sometimes, you might get home and realize you didn't understand something. You may need to talk to your source again.
5. Get the correct spelling of the person's name, as well as her title, if she has one. For example: Dr. Meg Stanford, Professor of Oceanography at Adams State University.

Facts from Research

Sometimes, you have to go to books, magazines, newspapers, and other reference sources to find facts to back up what you say. For example, the fact that 885 million people speak Chinese comes from an almanac.

When you wrote your research paper, you learned how to locate and use sources in the library and on the Internet. (If you need to, look back to Unit 2, Lesson 2.)

If you are looking for information on a local issue, check the library for back issues of your local newspaper. Or check to see if your local newspaper has an online edition. If it does, use its search function to see if there are stories about your topic.

Opposite Opinions

When you write an editorial, you know that others have different opinions. For example, the writer of the editorial arguing for more soccer fields knows that other people want the land to be used for more public parks instead.

When you research information for your editorial, take notes on facts and opinions that are different from yours. When you write your editorial, you will want to show that you are aware of these opposing arguments.

On the lines below, list two sources you plan to use for information and facts for your editorial. Your sources may be knowledgeable people or they may be printed sources, such as newspapers and almanacs.

_____

_____

_____

_____

Prewriting: Planning the Editorial

As in most writing, planning before you write will make your work stronger. For example, you may realize you are missing information, or that one of your arguments needs more evidence.

Here are points to consider as you plan your editorial.

Look at Your Evidence

The first step in planning your editorial is to look at the evidence you have gathered. Read through your notes and think about the opinion you are proving. If your evidence isn't strong, or doesn't support your thesis statement, you have two choices.

1. You can search for more information that supports your argument.

2. You can change your mind and take another point of view supported by the evidence you gathered.

Many writers find themselves in this situation. Don't be afraid to change your mind or go searching for more information. It's all part of the process.

Types of Supporting Evidence

Your editorial will be stronger if you offer different kinds of evidence to support your opinions. You already know about some types of evidence:

- Information from personal experience
- Facts from research in library sources
- Facts from interviews with experts and informed people
- Informed opinions from experts and people with first-hand knowledge

There are two other kinds of support you can use:

- Conclusions from facts. In Melissa's editorial, she writes, "Since there

is no other shelter in the area, without the Have-a-Heart Shelter they [the animals] would likely be destroyed." That sentence contains a fact: there is no other shelter in the area. A logical conclusion based on that fact is that without the shelter, animals may be destroyed.

- Opinions based on common experience. Sometimes, you don't need a fact from an expert to back up something most people will agree is true. For example, Melissa wrote, "The way a community cares for its most helpless residents, though, tells what that community is like." Most reasonable people would agree with that opinion.

As you plan your writing, think about the kinds of supporting evidence you can use. A good mix of evidence will make your writing more persuasive.

Make Your Plan

You have several choices for making a plan for writing your editorial. However you choose to make your plan, make sure that you include:

- *An introduction* that includes your thesis statement—a clear statement of what you are trying to persuade your audience to believe
- *A body* that tells background of the issue, if necessary, reasons and supporting information, and a solution, if you want to offer one
- *A conclusion* that reinforces your arguments and may urge your readers to action

Here are some ideas for how to make your plan:

A Web. If you are making a web to plan your essay, then each bubble that connects with the main idea in the middle should list a main point or reason. Under the reason you should write the supporting evidence, such as quotations, facts, and experiences. Here is what a web might look like for Melissa's editorial:

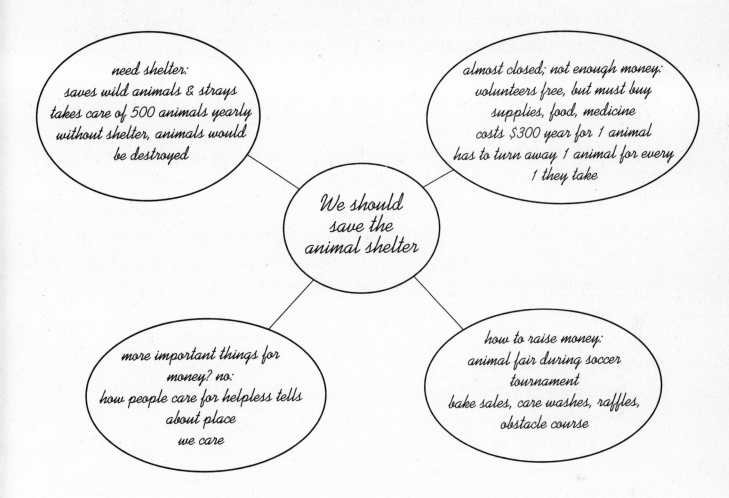

A Formal Outline. Here is how a formal outline might look for Melissa's editorial.

I. Introduction: Why save the shelter

II. Background: Shelter almost closed because of little money

    A. Shelter pays for food, medicine, supplies (volunteers work for free)

    B. Food for one animal is $300 year

    C. For every animal they take in, turn away another

III. We need the shelter

    A. Takes care of stray dogs and cats, wild animals

    B. Takes care of 300 animals a year

    C. Without shelter, many of these would be destroyed

IV. Good use of money? Yes—tells a community cares

V. How to raise money: "Animal Fair"

    A. Held during soccer tournament

    B. Bake sales, car washes, raffles, obstacle course

VI. Conclusion: As caring community, we must help

An Informal Outline. Some writers like the structure of outlining. Others think it slows them down. While formal outlining is necessary for a long research report, you can try an informal outline for your editorial. When you write an informal outline, you don't worry as much about making sure you follow the numbering system of a formal outline. You can just list your main points in order, followed by key words to remind you of the supporting facts and information. For example:

1. Introduction: Why save the shelter
2. Background—shelter almost closed because of little money
    -food, medicine, supplies, volunteers
3. Why we need the shelter
    -Takes care of stray dogs and cats, wild animals, 300 animals a year
4. Shelter shows that our community cares
5. Solution—raise money with "Animal Fair"
    -bake sales, car washes, raffles, obstacle course
6. Conclusion: As caring community, we must help

Use the space below and on the next page to plan your editorial. Make sure you include the supporting facts and information for each reason.

_____

_____

_____

_____

5

Drafting: Writing the Body

In most of the writing you have done this year, you have begun with the body and then written the introduction and conclusion. That's a good way to write your editorial, too. By the time you've written the body, you'll know better what to say in your introduction and conclusion.

As in many other kinds of nonfiction writing, when you write an editorial, you generally begin each paragraph with a topic sentence, followed by sentences that support the topic sentence. Read this paragraph from Melissa's editorial:

> Our town needs the shelter. The shelter takes care of injured wild animals as well as giving homes to stray cats and dogs. Keeping the shelter open is important—according to Dr. Moore, the shelter takes care of more than 500 animals a year. Since there is no other shelter in the area, without the Have-a-Heart Shelter these animals would likely be destroyed.

The topic sentence is *Our town needs the shelter.* The rest of the paragraph provides supporting evidence. Let's look at the sentences.

The shelter takes care of injured wild animals as well as giving homes to stray cats and dogs. That sentence is a fact. It states what the shelter does.

Keeping the shelter open is important—according to Dr. Moore, the shelter takes care of more than 500 animals a year. That sentence begins with Melissa's opinion—that it is important to keep the shelter open—and goes on to give a fact to support her opinion.

Since there is no other shelter in the area, without the Have-a-Heart Shelter these animals would likely be destroyed. That sentence is a logical conclusion based on a fact.

Considering Other Opinions

You might think that the best way to convince your reader is to give all the evidence you can find for your opinion and leave out any arguments against it. However, you will be much more convincing if you state the main arguments against your opinion, and then show the problems with those arguments.

Reread this paragraph from Melissa's editorial. She knew some people would rather donate money to other causes, so she addressed that argument in this paragraph:

> Some people say that there are more important things to donate their money to. It's true, there are many good causes worthy of support, such as the Friends of the Library and the Jefferson Area Food Bank. But the way a community cares for its most helpless residents, animals as well as people, tells what that community is like. By raising money to help care for animals that have been abandoned, or are wild and injured, we show that we are a caring community.

She makes her overall argument stronger by including that paragraph, in which she writes what opponents might say, and counters their argument.

Begin Writing

You have all the tools you need to write: your thesis sentence, your plan, your notes, and your beliefs. Now, write the first draft of the body. Remember, in this first draft, don't worry too much about spelling, punctuation, and other details. Focus your attention on making your points in order and providing convincing evidence.

When you write your draft, double-space to leave room for revisions later.

Drafting: Writing the Introduction and Conclusion

Do you remember the main jobs of an introduction and conclusion to an essay? In general, an introduction should

- Interest your reader,
- Tell what you are writing about

A conclusion should

- Wrap up what you are writing about,
- Give the reader something to think about

When you write an editorial, your introduction and conclusion should do not only those jobs but other jobs as well.

Introducing the Editorial

The introduction to your editorial should clearly state the problem or issue and your opinion about it. It should include your thesis statement. Notice that Melissa decided to get her audience's attention by stating the problem, and ended with her thesis statement. Read Melissa's introduction again:

The Have-a-Heart Animal Shelter is in trouble. Last month, the shelter's board of directors announced that the shelter might have to close unless more donations come in. Last week the Jefferson Area Youth Soccer League raised more than $5,000 for the shelter. This was a good start, but it is only a beginning. The shelter is important for our community, and we need to do more to make sure that it stays open.

1. What problem does Melissa identify?

_____

_____

2. What is Melissa's opinion?

_____

_____

Write Your Introduction

Now it's time to write your introduction. Remember, clearly describe the problem or issue, and state your opinion about it. Double-space to leave room for revisions later.

Concluding the Editorial

The conclusion to an editorial is your last chance to persuade your reader. You can do this in these ways:

- Restate the argument. You can use different wording to express your opinion so your reader looks at it in a new way. Here is an example Melissa used: "As people who care about animals and our community, it is our job to make sure the shelter stays open." She is restating her original opinion that "we need to do more to make sure the shelter stays open."

- Issue a call to action. Melissa's ending recommends an action based on her opinion: she asks her audience to raise money to save the shelter. A call to action will not be appropriate for every editorial, but it can be effective to recommend something for your reader to do.

Write Your Conclusion

Now it's time to write your conclusion. Do your best to make your reader agree with you. Double-space to leave room for revisions later.

Revising: Improving the Editorial

Your first draft—introduction, body, and conclusion—is complete. Now it's time to revise your work and make it as good as it can be. Look at each of these elements of your editorial in turn.

Content and Organization

Read your editorial. Did you include the major points you wanted to make? Can you easily follow the arguments in the editorial? Does your editorial move smoothly from point to point?

Watch Your Tone

The *tone* of an essay is the sense of a voice that comes through the words. When you write a persuasive essay, such as an editorial, you need to be careful about your tone. Especially if you feel very strongly about your opinions, then you need to be careful not to let your tone get too emotional.

Be careful not to attack those who disagree with you, or pass judgments that aren't backed up with evidence. For example, imagine that the following sentences appeared in Melissa's editorial:

> If the people of this town don't support the shelter, they're just selfish. Some people say there are more important things to spend money on, but they are just wrong.

The first statement insults people who don't support the shelter. It is likely to make those people angry instead of persuading them. Name-calling is no way to win an editorial argument. A more effective way of persuading someone is to write reasons that make sense, and support them with facts.

The second statement passes a strict judgment on people who disagree with the writer. But often, opinions are not right or wrong—they are just different. You are better off explaining why your opinion is right rather than claiming someone else is wrong.

Another problem editorial writers sometimes have is overstating their evidence. Here are a couple of examples that might have appeared in Melissa's editorial.

Thousands of dogs will die without the shelter!
Everyone knows the shelter is important.

In the first sentence, the writer is overstating the case—unless she can *prove* that thousands of dogs will die. In your eagerness to make your point, be certain you can prove what you write.

In the second statement, notice the word *everyone*. Watch out for words like *everyone, never, no one,* and *always*. Proving that everyone thinks something or no one does something is very difficult. Avoid such absolute statements. Instead, use words and phrases like *most people* or *in general*.

Incorrect Generalizations

A common problem with editorials is reasoning that because something happened to you or someone you know, it is generally true. For example, you might write that you rode your bicycle without a helmet and didn't get into an accident—which proves that riding a bike without a helmet is safe. But your individual experience is not a very strong argument, because someone else could have a very different experience that is equally true. Look closely at your use of personal examples as evidence to make sure you don't make sweeping generalizations.

Paragraphs and Sentences

As you revise, look at your paragraphs and sentences.

Make sure your introduction:
- Clearly states your opinion
- Catches the attention of your reader

Make sure each paragraph in the body:

- Is about one main idea that helps prove your opinion
- Has a topic sentence that explains what the paragraph will be about
- Has sentences with examples, facts, explanations, and information from experts that prove the topic sentence

Make sure the conclusion:

- Wraps up your argument
- Makes a strong effort to convince your reader

When you have finished, read through your paper again. Are you convinced by what you wrote? If so, your revision is finished.

Proofreading and Publishing: Finishing the Editorial

Your editorial is almost finished. After you complete one last check, you can make your final copy. This time, you are checking for the details.

Grammar

Check that each sentence is complete, with a subject and a verb.

Make sure sentences are not run-on or fragments.

Punctuation

Make sure every sentence ends with the correct punctuation mark.

Check your use of commas, apostrophes, and quotation marks.

Spelling

Check the spelling of words you are unsure of.

Check proper names to make sure each is spelled correctly.

Make a clean final copy. When you are sure that everything is correct, you are finished!

Publishing

Read aloud your editorial to family and friends. If you wrote your editorial about something that concerns your community, you can send it to your local newspaper as a letter to the editor.

WRITING A SPEECH

Choosing a Topic for a Speech

Understanding Speeches

What do these have in common?

- A President gives the State of the Union address.
- A cooking teacher tells her class how to make an omelet.
- An animal lover urges a group to give money to save prairie dogs.

They are all speeches. On many occasions you may be called upon to give a speech. Some might be informal—for example, when someone delivers remarks at a wedding to congratulate the new bride and groom. Others will be formal, and need preparation and practice, such as a presentation to the directors of a business.

In this unit, you will plan and write a speech. Then you will deliver it and learn the great feeling that comes from having people listen attentively to what *you* have to say.

Knowing Your Audience and Purpose

How you write your speech depends in part on your audience. Imagine, for instance, that you are giving a speech about an artist you like. You would give one speech to a group of art historians. You would give a different speech to a group of eight-year-olds about to take a museum tour. When you write your speech, you need to think about the people you'll be addressing, and write as if you were speaking directly to that audience.

Depending on the occasion and the audience, writers design speeches to achieve different purposes. Here are some different types of speeches:

Informative. An informative speech gives the audience new information. For example, you might give a speech to inform visitors to a museum about the life of a particular artist.

Persuasive. A persuasive speech is designed to convince the audience to agree with your opinions about an issue or convince the audience to take action. For example, a politician might give a speech to persuade voters to vote for her.

Entertaining. An entertaining speech entertains the audience. For example, you might entertain an audience by telling the story of a camping trip in which nothing turned out as you planned.

Once you know the kind of speech you will deliver, you can focus your writing so the people in your audience will respond as you want them to. For instance, if you are writing an informative speech about how to use a fishing rod, you will want to make your directions as clear as possible so your audience will be able to use the rod. If you are writing to persuade, you want to include convincing evidence so your audience ends up agreeing with you.

Read about the following speeches. On each line, write if the speech is *persuasive, informative,* or *entertaining.*

1. _____ A speech that tells the funny things that happened in the house when mom was gone for a weekend.

2. _____ A speech about the migration of monarch butterflies from Mexico to the United States.

3. _____ A speech about ancient Rome.

4. _____ A speech by a congresswoman about how the medical research budget should be larger.

5. _____ A speech about how to make an apple pie.

Reading a Speech

Read the following informative speech, delivered by a student named Rory to fellow members of his Scouting troop. Rory was asked to give a speech about doing something he knows well.

Imagine you're sitting outside, watching the sun turn the mountain peaks purple. You hear the lonely cry of an owl across the lake. Over a warm campfire, the marshmallow you're roasting turns golden brown. That's backpacking at its best. When you go backpacking, there are no cars, no computers, no refrigerators—it's just you, your friends, the wilderness, and whatever you can carry on your back. You can have a wonderful backpacking experience if you carefully prepare for your trip by choosing the right place to camp, and, most of all, by bringing the right equipment.

First, how do you find a good place to go backpacking? There are several types of camping spots, but I'm going to focus on two: state and national parks. If you want to go to a state park, you can call the state parks department or go to the library to find a directory that describes where you can camp. If you want to backpack in a national park, you need to reserve a spot before you go. National parks are so beautiful and popular that many people want to backpack through them. So, to keep the park from getting too crowded, only a certain number of people are allowed to stay overnight. You need to reserve a camping spot, and you can do this through the Internet.

Once you know where you're going, you'll need to pack the right equipment. Here are four basic items you need for a successful backpacking trip. First, you need a sleeping bag that will keep you warm if the weather gets cold. Second, you need a roll-up camping pad to cushion you when you are sleeping. Third, you need a tent that can hold you and the people you're camping with. Fourth, you need a good backpack. You'll need one that is sturdier and larger than the backpacks you might use for books. So, the basic equipment you need includes a sleeping bag, a pad, a tent, and a backpack.

You will also need to pack a few other items. For cooking, you will need a mess kit, which has a plate, bowl, utensils, and frying pan. You also need matches to start a fire. Keep your matches in a waterproof container, because if they get wet, they won't light! Always bring a good first aid kit, a flashlight with extra batteries, insect repellant, and a whistle. Why a whistle? If you get separated from your friends, you can blow the whistle to help them find you.

Don't forget some of the most important equipment of all: food and water. Bring a full water bottle because you'll get thirsty doing all that exploring. But water is heavy! Many backpackers also bring a small water filter so they can drink stream water. Remember, there are no refrigerators in the wilderness, so don't pack ice cream or any other food that needs to stay cold. Instead, pack foods that are light to carry and only need water to cook, like pasta and instant oatmeal.

So, you have your sleeping bag, a tent, cooking utensils, an emergency kit, food, and water. Now all you need is your clothes. There are two rules for clothing: pack light and layer. A winter coat is heavy and hard to carry. So bring a windproof jacket, a warm sweater, a long sleeved shirt, and a short sleeved shirt instead, as well as a pair of shorts. They're easy to carry, and you can change clothes as the weather changes.

Now you're all set for your backpacking trip. You've reserved a place to stay and rounded up the equipment you need, from sleeping bag to first aid kit. You've packed food and water. You've brought clothes you can layer. Can't you just imagine yourself in a beautiful, wild place as the sun sets across the lake, listening to the owls and the crackling fire? You're going to have a wonderful time.

1. What is the main point of Rory's speech?

_____

_____

2. How does Rory engage the listener's interest in his opening paragraph?

_____

_____

_____

3. What are Rory's suggestions for finding a place to camp? How does he organize this part of his speech?

_____

_____

_____

Choosing a Topic

Now, you'll choose a topic for an informative speech. The topic should be something you know well. Remember that you are not trying to tell a story or persuade someone. Instead, you are informing your audience about something they might not know. Rory, who wrote the speech you just read, knew about backpacking because he had gone many times with his family.

Here are some possibilities that might spark an idea for you:

Hobbies
making model airplanes
cooking
sewing
gardening
art

Talents you have developed
singing
playing an instrument
acting
dancing
karate

Interests
pets
fishing
choosing a good book to read
computers
music

Travel and other places
places you've been on
    vacation
the state or town in which
    you live
places your relatives live
the place you moved from

What you've been studying
history
science
literature
geography

Games
chess
video games
board games
outdoor games

Sports
soccer
baseball
gymnastics

If none of those ideas helps you think of a topic for your speech, look through your writing journal, if you keep one, for possibilities. You can also try freewriting. Set a timer for ten minutes. Take a sheet of paper, and for that time, write about what interests you—not in sentences, but in words and phrases. At the end of the ten minutes, look at what you wrote. See if something grabs your interest.

Narrowing Your Topic

Your idea should be narrow enough to write a short speech about. Rory's speech is about three to four minutes long. Writing a three-minute speech about pets—and covering all the important parts of the topic—would be hard to do. The topic of caring for a new puppy would be much easier to cover in a three-minute speech.

Like the chair that Goldilocks picks in the bears' cottage, you want your topic to be not too big, not too small, but just right. If you have too much to cover, narrow your topic: think of a way you could write about the same topic, but in a smaller way. Practice by narrowing any two of the topics below.

1. outer space

_____

2. computers

_____

3. books for children

_____

4. weather

_____

5. wild animals

_____

Developing Subtopics

One you have picked and narrowed the topic for your speech, you need to think more about what you want to say. Rory decided to start by making a list of the things someone who wanted to go backpacking would need to know. Notice that the list isn't in order. At first, Rory was just trying to get his ideas down.

what kind of food you need

gathering firewood

clothing--not too heavy

bring a whistle

layer your clothing

where to find a camping place

state and national parks—make a reservation!

waterproof shoes

what backpacking is!

what kind of equipment you need--tent, sleeping bag

different kinds of pads

get up early to see sun

other equipment you need, like matches, flashlight, first aid kit

water bottle and purifier

don't bring heavy coat

Later, Rory examined his list and organized it into subtopics for his speech.

On the lines below, write the most important things someone listening to you needs to know about your topic. You will use some of what you write as subtopics for your speech. Don't worry about writing your ideas in any particular order; just get down as many ideas as you can think of.

_____

_____

_____

_____

_____

_____

_____

_____

Writing a Thesis Statement

Now you have a good idea of what your speech will contain. You can use this information to help you write a thesis statement.

Your thesis statement will tell your audience what you will be talking about. You will include your thesis statement in your introduction to let your audience know the subject of your speech.

When Rory examined his list of subtopics, he noticed that most of his ideas were about how to prepare for a backpacking trip, including choosing a place and, most of all, gathering the right equipment.

Here is the thesis statement in Rory's introduction:

> You can have a wonderful experience if you carefully prepare for your trip by choosing the right place to camp, and, most of all, bringing the right equipment.

The rest of Rory's speech tells about the preparations a backpacker needs to make for a good camping experience, with a focus on the right equipment.

Examine your list of subtopics. What seems to stand out most? What main idea emerges from the things you listed?

On the lines below, write a draft of your thesis statement.

_____

_____

_____

_____

_____

_____

_____

_____

Planning and Writing the Speech

Deciding Purpose and Audience

When you give a speech, it helps to know your audience and why are you are speaking to them. Before you write your speech, think about these questions:

- **What is my purpose?** You are writing an informative speech. That means you will be telling people information they might not know but that might be useful, helpful, or interesting to them. For example, Rory's speech would be helpful to anyone who has wanted to try backpacking. On the lines below, write your purpose.

_____

_____

_____

- **Who is my audience?** If you are writing a speech to deliver to people who know something about your topic, you can use terms they will already know. For example, if Rory's speech was to people who already know about backpacking, he could talk about a mess kit and not have to explain what it is. Since Rory is speaking to people who are new to backpacking, he needs to explain what a mess kit is. On the lines below, write who you your audience is.

_____

_____

_____

_____

Answer these questions about your audience.

• What do they already know about my topic?

_____

_____

• What would they like to know about my topic?

_____

_____

When you know the answers to those questions, you will be able to write your speech with your audience in mind, as if you were talking directly to someone listening.

Making a Plan

Once you have a topic, you need to decide what to say about it. You have used a web before to help you plan, and that may work well for planning this speech, too. To make his web, Rory looked at the list of subtopics he made. Then he circled the ones he thought were most important. His web looked like this:

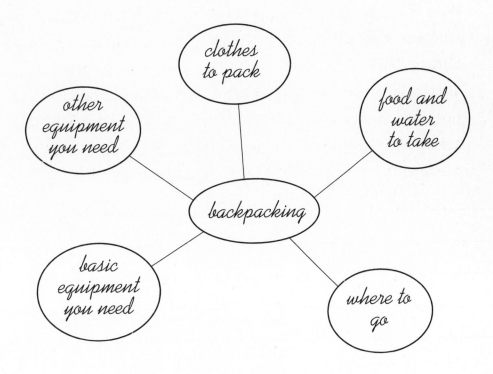

Look at your list of subtopics to help you make your web. Use the space below. You may need more or fewer bubbles than Rory used for the main points you will make.

topic of speech:

music

Writing an Outline

Now, turn your plan into an outline. An outline will help you write a speech that is well-organized and easy for your listeners to understand. You have already written outlines. Here is a brief review of how an outline looks:

I. Introduction
II. Body
  A. Main point
        1. Supporting information
        2. Supporting information
  B. Main Point
        1.Supporting information
        2. Supporting information
III. Conclusion

Your outline may have more main points and supporting information, depending on what you plan to say. Look at the web you made. You can use this to help you write an outline. Decide the order in which you will present your main points. Rory's main points, based on his web, are:

- Planning a place to camp
- Basic equipment to bring
- Other equipment to bring
- Food and water to bring
- Clothing to bring

Under each of your main points, write the information you have that supports that main point. Look again at the list of subtopics you made. You may find information there that you can use.

Writing for Listeners

Writing a speech is a little different from writing a letter or report. In this case, your audience is listening, not reading. Think about the differences between when you listen for information and when you read for information. As you read, you can go back to something you didn't quite get, or read it a couple of times before you understand it. When you listen, you only get one chance to understand.

Here are some tips for writing speeches:

- Write simply. Don't write long sentences that might be confusing. Use language you know your audience will understand.

- Make sure you begin every paragraph with a topic sentence that clearly explains what you will be talking about. That helps your reader follow along and know exactly where he is being taken, step by step. For example, Rory begins one of his paragraphs with this topic sentence: "Don't forget some of the most important equipment of all: food and water." His listeners know that now he will talk about food and water for backpacking.

- Sometimes, it helps to tell your listeners what you are about to say before you say it. For instance, in Rory's speech, he said, "There are several types of camping spots, but I'm going to focus on two: state and national parks." Rory's listeners know what to expect next, which helps them get ready to hear and understand it. Rory also wrote: "Here are four basic items you need for a successful backpacking trip." The words "Here are four basic items" clue the listener to listen for four things. Rory follows that by labeling each thing, "First," "Second," "Third," and "Fourth":

> *First*, you need a sleeping bag that will keep you warm if the weather gets cold. *Second*, you need a roll-up camping pad to cushion you when you are sleeping. *Third,* you need a tent that can hold you and the people you are camping with. *Fourth*, you need a good backpack.

- Restate your main points. Rory wrote a paragraph about basic backpacking equipment. At the end of the paragraph, he wrote: "So, the basic equipment you need includes a sleeping bag, a pad, a tent, and a backpack." That is helpful to listeners who want to keep track of Rory's advice.

- Write clear transitions. Words such as *next, then,* and *finally* help guide your listener from one point to another, and make it easier to follow what you are saying.

Developing a Speech Style

Most listeners enjoy hearing a speech that sounds more like a conversation, and less like a written page. Read the following two sentences aloud. Which would sound better in a speech, and be more effective?

The English springer spaniel is not only a great hunter, but a great companion, too.

The English springer spaniel breed, long beloved by hunters for its ability to retrieve, is also popular with those seeking a pet.

The first sentence is more informal and more like a conversation. It tries to connect with the listener. The second sentence sounds more formal. While it might be fine for an essay, it would not be as effective in a speech.

Writing the Body

You have the outline of the main points you want to make, as well as the supporting information for each main point. You're set to write the body of your speech. (After you write the body, you will write the introduction and conclusion.)

On a separate sheet of paper, write a draft of the body of your speech. Double-space to leave room for revisions.

Writing the Introduction

The introduction to a speech has two jobs: to interest your reader and to tell him what you will be speaking about (your thesis statement).

When you begin speaking, you have a short time to capture and hold the interest of your listener. One way *not* to begin is, "In my speech, I will be talking about . . . " That is likely to lose your listeners' interest.

Here are some ways to catch their interest:

The Vivid Description: Rory's speech begins with a vivid description. He paints a scene that makes a listener want to hear more.

The Question: You can begin with a question that interests your audience enough to want to know the answer. Rory might have begun his speech with: "Do you ever feel like you'd just like to leave your cares behind and get away from it all?"

The Startling Statement: If you tell your audience something that surprises them, they will listen to find out more. Rory might have written this opening: "Each year, hundreds of thousands of people leave behind their jobs, their homes, and their families, and head for the woods. Not to become hermits, but for a few days of refreshing backpacking."

The Memorable Quotation: This can be a trickier for a speech than for a paper. Make sure any quotation you use is short and easy to understand, as well as being memorable. For example, Rory might have begun his essay like this:

> The poet Edmund Blunden wrote, "I am for the woods against the world." When you start to feel that way, ready to leave the world behind and head for the woods, then the best thing to do is strap on a backpack and start walking.

A Little-Known Fact: Sometimes, you can grab your listeners' interest by telling them an interesting fact or something they may not know about a common subject. For example: "In our National Parks, there are more than 125,000 square miles of spectacular scenery—and the best way to see it is to backpack."

On a separate sheet, write a draft of the introduction to your speech. Try one of the approaches above. You may want to try more than one, and choose the one you like best.

Writing the Conclusion

Your conclusion should sum up your speech and leave your listener with a sense that he or she understands the main points of what you set out to tell. Finally, leave your listener with an image or idea that will wrap up the speech. Reread Rory's conclusion:

> Now you're all set for your backpacking trip. You've reserved a place to stay and rounded up the equipment you need, from sleeping bag to first aid kit. You've packed food and water. You've brought clothes you can layer. Can't you just imagine yourself in a beautiful, wild place as the sun sets across the lake, listening to the owls and the crackling fire? You're going to have a wonderful time.

Notice how Rory briefly restates the main points of his speech, and ends with an image that recalls the introduction of the speech. His listeners will go home feeling they have learned something.

On a separate sheet, write a draft of your conclusion.

Revising and Proofreading the Speech

Revising the Speech

Because a speech is meant to be read aloud and listened to, the best way to know what needs to be revised is to read it aloud to yourself. There is a real difference between how a speech sounds in your head and what it sounds like when you read it aloud. Reading aloud can help you find places in the speech where you

- Realize that an idea doesn't belong
- Realize you are missing an important idea
- Need to add transitions between ideas or sentences
- Use the same word or phrase too often
- Need to reword to make something clearer
- Need to reword because a sentence is too long or complicated
- Find yourself stumbling over an awkward sentence

After you make the revisions, deliver your speech to another person. That will help you gain yet another perspective on what works and what doesn't. Notice how your listener responds. If she is interested, she will lean forward and keep her eyes on yours. If she is confused, you will see that on her face, too.

When you finish reading your speech to a practice audience, ask your audience these questions, and listen carefully to the answers:

- What did you like best?
- What didn't you think worked well?
- What did you find confusing?
- Were you able to follow the speech from point to point?
- What was the main thing you learned from the speech? (If your listener can't tell you what she learned, or learned something you didn't think was important, it's time to revise!)
- Did your attention wander at all? When?

Use the answers from your listener to help you make revisions.

Proofreading the Speech

Before you are ready to prepare a final copy of your speech, proofread for:

- Grammar

  Are any of the sentences run-on?

  Do all subjects and verbs agree?

- Mechanics

  Are words capitalized correctly?

  Does every sentence have an end mark?

  Are punctuation marks used correctly?

- Spelling

  Are words spelled correctly?

  Are proper names spelled correctly?

When you have corrected any errors, make a clean final copy of your speech.

Delivering the Speech

Preparing Notes

By carefully preparing to deliver your speech, when you step up to talk you will feel confident, appear professional, and impress your audience with your poise and your knowledge.

In general, it is more effective to deliver a short speech from memory, rather than reading aloud the final draft. Your speech will sound more natural, and your listeners will be more engaged. You can make eye contact with your listeners if you are not looking down at a paper.

You can prepare some notes to help you remember your speech and prompt you along the way.

Gather a 4 x 6 index card. On this card, you'll write the main points of your speech. These should be the same as the main points in your outline, but in case you discovered a new point or direction while writing your speech, make sure to check your speech as well. On each card, write brief phrases that you will remember. Here's the way Rory's note card looked:

- intro: descrip. of mountains & sunset

    what is backpacking

    prepare carefully: place and the equipment
- finding a place: state and national parks, reserving spot
- basic equipment: sleeping bag, pad, tent, backpack
- other equipment: mess kit, first aid, matches, flashlight, repellant, whistle
- food and water: filter, pack light, instant products, no refrig
- packing clothes: layer and pack light
- conclusion: made all preparations--imagine yourself in beautiful place

---

Remember, this note card is just to remind you of what comes next, if you forget. But you probably won't forget if you practice so much that you know your speech well.

Practicing the Speech

If you practice until you know your speech by heart, you will be able to concentrate on what you are saying, and how you are saying it. Knowing your speech will give you confidence, too.

Memorize your speech a bit at a time. Start by reading it through aloud once. Then work on each paragraph, memorizing one and then moving to the next. Every time you memorize a paragraph, start from the beginning and give the speech as far as you have it memorized. It won't take too long until you know the whole speech.

Once you know your speech by heart, you can work on your delivery. Try delivering it once in front of a mirror. Here are some things to remember when you are delivering a speech.

- **Eye contact.** Find a friendly face in the audience, and talk to that person. Doing that helps you connect with your audience, and makes public speaking a little less scary, since you are speaking to one, not many. When you feel comfortable, make eye contact with others in the audience.

- **Posture.** Stand up straight and you will look more confident and show you have something worthwhile to say. Try it yourself. Stand up straight and say the first sentence of your speech. Now hunch over and say the same sentence. Which presentation do you think will make a better impression on your audience?

- **Speaking Style.** Don't mumble. Speak loudly enough to be heard. Speak clearly, and not too fast. Practice the first paragraph of your speech, paying particular attention to speaking loudly, clearly, and not too fast. If you start speaking this way, continuing the same way will be easier.

- **Expression.** Because you know your speech so well, you can work on your expression—the way you deliver funny lines, the tone of your voice, the smiles and looks that will add to your audience's understanding of what you say.

- **Gestures.** If you gesture when something is particularly important, your audience will pay more attention to the words you are saying, and will understand they should pay more attention. When you gesture, don't overdo it. Just do it as you would in a conversation. Also, remember not to gesture unless you are making a point. Twisting a lock of hair or putting your hands to your mouth will distract your audience. Unless you are gesturing for a reason, keep your arms relaxed and at your side.

Avoiding Stage Fright

Giving a speech makes some people nervous. If you are one of these people, the best way to deal with nervousness is to practice your speech so much that you could almost give it in your sleep.

Make sure you practice giving your speech several times before you present it to your audience. Knowing the material well builds confidence. Also, remember that on your subject, you are the expert. People are listening to you because of what you know.

Delivering the Speech

You are ready to deliver your speech. Before you do, take three deep breaths. Have your note card ready. Remember to look out at your audience. Remember that you are the expert on this topic and that the people in the audience want to hear what you have to say. You'll give a great speech.